HINDSIGHT

Also by Kate Hart Nardone
Pieces of an Abstract Hart

HINDSIGHT

Looking Back with Godly Perspective

A Devotional

By Kate Hart Nardone

XULON PRESS

Xulon Press
2301 Lucien Way #415
Maitland, FL 32751
407.339.4217
www.xulonpress.com

Editing by: Charissa Ricketts and Barbara Hart

Cover design by: Kate Hart Nardone and Drew Lawton

Unless otherwise indicated, Scripture quotations taken from the King James Version (KJV)–public domain.

Scripture quotations taken from The Message (MSG). Copyright © 1993, 1994, 1995, 1996, 2000, 2001, 2002. Used by permission of NavPress Publishing Group. Used by permission. All rights reserved.

Scripture quotations taken from the Holy Bible, New International Version (NIV). Copyright © 1973, 1978, 1984, 2011 by Biblica, Inc.™. Used by permission. All rights reserved.

Scripture quotations taken from the Contemporary English Version (CEV). Copyright © 1995 American Bible Society. Used by permission. All rights reserved.

Scripture quotations taken from the English Standard Version (ESV). Copyright © 2001 by Crossway, a publishing ministry of Good News Publishers. Used by permission. All rights reserved.

Scripture quotations taken from the Amplified Bible (AMP). Copyright © 1954, 1958, 1962, 1964, 1965, 1987 by The Lockman Foundation. Used by permission. All rights reserved.

Scripture quotations taken from The Holy Bible, Berean Study Bible (BSB). Copyright ©2016, 2018 by Bible Hub. Used by Permission. All Rights Reserved Worldwide.

Printed in the United States of America.

ISBN-13: 978-1-6312-9543-0

My earthly journey began in 1982 when God gave me to my parents, Harold and Barbara Hart.

Thank you both for your love, Biblical instruction, discipline, forgiveness, and encouragement. I am the woman I am because you taught me to believe in Jesus and because you believed in me.

Daddy, thank you for my name, which means "purity." I know that through Jesus' blood, all the stains of my life have been washed clean.

Mom, you are my friend and mentor. You practice what you preach. You are my Proverbs 31 woman.

Thank you both for training me up in the way I should go; thank you for the wisdom passed to me over the years. I love you both more than any words could express. I consider myself divinely favored for being yours.

I dedicate this book to you, with a heart full of gratitude.

"O Master, there are the conditions in which people live, and yes, in these very conditions my spirit is alive – fully recovered with a fresh infusion of life! It seems it was good for me to go through all those troubles. Throughout them all You held tight to my lifeline. You never let me tumble over the edge into nothing. But my sins You let go of, threw them over Your shoulder – good riddance!"

Isaiah 38:16-17 (MSG)

Table of Contents

Acknowledgements

THERE ARE NO WORDS THAT CAN EXPRESS THE LOVE and thanks I have for the many people God has placed in my life, who have helped make this book become a reality.

Matt, thank you for your encouragement, your faith in my writing, and your financial help along the way. God knew I needed you before I did and orchestrated the events in our lives that put us together. You are not just my husband; you are my soulmate. I love you.

Matthew, Christian, Trinity and Kairi – my beautiful children. Without you, these pages would have less color and meaning. You inspire me every day in so many ways. You are the jewels in my crown.

Megan Hart, Marie Virella and Charissa Ricketts – thank you for your honesty and constructive criticism. This book turned out the way it did because of your candor and your generous help.

Kevin McGarvey and Rebecca Bonham – thank you both for the PUSH. You saw things in me that I didn't see in myself. Your encouragement in my life and your belief in my work has allowed me to shed the fear and just go for it!

Pastors Woodson Moore, Rita Patrick, Jamie Morgan, Ralph Snook, and Ken Corson – you have been my teachers. Thank you for the individual ways you have all hidden the Word of God deep in my heart, and the way you have all challenged and grown me.

Pastor Paul Scull, Patti Felsburg and Thor Knutstad – thank you for listening. Thank you for allowing me to be transparent and vulnerable with you, and for keeping me safe throughout.

Paula Sheets, Barbara Nichols, Christine Strittmatter, Doris Wilson, Garnett and George Glenning, Ted and Dee Coyle – thank you all for your spiritual parenting. Thank you for seeing something in this rebel, and for loving me when I was unlovable. I will never forget.

To all the staff at Xulon Press – thank you for walking with me through the process with love and patience. You have been a blessing. I pray God sends each of you the ten-fold return for all you've done.

Marc Bermudez, my production rep and friend – thank you for the connections and the way you have always believed in me. Twenty years ago, I never would have thought we would be doing this together. I'm honored.

To all my friends and mentors who have contributed to the stories of my life and to the principles I share in this book, thank you. You know who you are, and I love you dearly. It is my prayer that you will find the satisfaction and fulfillment in life that I have found by obeying God and completing this work.

When I look back on the story of my life, I know I have been fortunate enough to grow up in a family of unbelievably strong people. I did not come to realize this because life has been blissful. I have learned this through tear-filled eyes that have seen the devastation of life assault with little mercy, the same eyes that have watched the phoenixes rise from the ashes with dignity and beauty. To my grandparents, parents, siblings, aunts, uncles, cousins, nieces, and nephews – you all have your own stories of extreme hardship to tell, all not realizing the pride I have in the way each of you has carried on through every heartbreak. You are all the branches of a family tree, rooted in strength and love. You are my heroes. Mommom Stella, it all started with you. 'Thank you' is not enough.

Author's Preface

HINDSIGHT DID NOT BEGIN AS A DEVOTIONAL. I began writing down these memories to use one day in a memoir. After reading over the stories several times, the Lord spoke to me and gave me the word "hindsight." I began to study its deeper meaning, and suddenly I understood what He was asking me to do–look at the stories of my life through Godly perspective to see what I have learned, what has changed, and how to encourage others. The seed was planted in my heart and mind at that moment, and the journey of writing this devotional began.

God has been faithful to strengthen my faith and give me courage to share with you some of the best and worst times of my life, the constant thread always being that He was there with me.

I arranged these devotions with the guidance of the Holy Spirit's direction, through the Word. Among the stories, I have also included several dreams the Lord has given me, as well as the interpretations. There is a common theme of kindness and compassion; other topics stand alone. At the end of each story or dream, I have placed the hindsight lesson I personally learned, followed by an encouragement to the reader. You will find Scripture and cohesive quotes paired throughout.

It is my desire that you can take away something valuable from these lessons and develop a deeper understanding for how unconditionally loved you are.

May you also look back at the milestone moments, people and places of your life, and have Godly perspective in reflection as well.

Life is hard, but God is good.

1
Unexpected Acceptance

"Compassion will cure more sins than condemnation."
-Henry Ward Beecher

WHEN I WAS YOUNG, MY FATHER HAD A BEST FRIEND named Dan Wright, Sr. He worked in the local school system as a vice principal, taught Sunday School at our church, and was a devoted husband and loving father and grandfather.

He watched me grow up from a baby to young adult. There were many versions of 'Kate' he got to witness over the years. Some, I am proud of…many, not so much. I imagine my father must have confided in him about me over the years. He had to have known some pretty ugly things about me.

In all the years I had the honor of knowing him, he never once treated me unkindly. He always said the same three words every time he saw me. In fact, he made sure he never missed the opportunity to say them.

"I like you."

That was it. Three simple words. The same three words he spoke to me during my best years, my worst years, and everything in between. Sometimes they made sense to me. Sometimes they confused me. But I always knew they were coming. He never failed to deliver them.

He never took me aside to praise me in any other way. He never felt the need to correct me, when I deserved to be put in my place. Always just a smile and three consistent words.

We lost my Uncle Danny to cancer in 2009. I was 26 years old at the time. As I walked over to view him at the service, I touched his hand, leaned over and said, "I like you, too."

Hindsight:

I know this story was a simple one, but it is so important. You see, during a huge part of my life, I was lost and very insecure. I didn't even like myself. I knew that I had people who loved me, but my Uncle Danny was the only person that ever greeted or departed from me by saying he liked me. You can love someone without liking them. To a messed-up kid who was looking for acceptance, knowing I was liked was far more valuable than being loved. Being liked was being seen and being accepted. That was what I needed, and he knew that. Those three small kind words will stay with me my entire life.

**"Accept one another, then, just as Christ accepted you,
in order to bring praise to God."
Romans 15:7 (NIV)**

Your words have power. Power to build up and power to destroy. I'm sure right now, you can immediately think of an unkind thing someone said to you in the past. Often, remembering those words instantly brings on negative feelings and emotions. That is because the famous "sticks and stones" saying is utter garbage. Words can absolutely hurt you. Not only can they hurt, they can destroy.

What will you choose to do with your words? Will you use them as a weapon, or will you use them to speak life into people? Yes, they are that powerful! They can literally save someone's life or push them over the edge. So, bless people with your words. Be kind with them. Be thoughtful with them. Be loving and accepting with them. Use them to comfort. Use them to encourage. Use them to show others their value and worth. Ask God to give you opportunities. He will.

"You can change a life by touching someone with simple, beautiful, kind words and a loving smile."
-Debasish Mridha

2

Finding Purpose

"For I know the plans I have for you," declares the
Lord, "plans to prosper you and not to harm you,
plans to give you hope and a future."
Jeremiah 29:11 (NIV)

IT WAS A COLD DAY IN THE WINTER OF 2002. MY
hands were dry and cracked, wrapped tightly around the steering
wheel of my '91 Ford Taurus. I was wandering around in my car
with no direction; I just knew I couldn't go home yet. I wish I knew
exactly what I was thinking about, but the stress level washed it
from my memory. I just know I was lost. Not lost in the sense that
I didn't know where I was; I just didn't know where I was going
(in more ways than one).

At one point, something took over my steering. Sounds crazy,
I know; it didn't make sense to me either. Before I knew it, my
car ended up in the parking lot of Chestnut Assembly of God (a
church one town over from where I lived). I sat in the parking lot
for a while, staring at the big concrete cross that runs the full top
to bottom length of the building. It comforted and scared me at
the same time. I got out slowly and started walking toward the

entrance. I didn't see any other cars in the parking lot, so for all I knew the building was locked...but it wasn't. I opened the door, but held it open for a minute. My hands were shaking, but not from the cold. I knew the moment I touched those doors that the presence of God was in this building, and it made me tremble. Holding that door in limbo, I faced the biggest decision of my life. I needed to step IN or back OUT.

Let me briefly explain my life and challenges at the time before I continue:

When I found out I was pregnant with my son, I was not in any way prepared to be a mom. I was 19, in an unhealthy relationship, not making good decisions, and was very self-destructive. I had attempted suicide once already and was struggling every day to choose to be alive. I was lost and finding comfort in the wrong people and in the wrong things.

Regardless of all that, I wanted my baby from the second I found out he existed. Even though he wasn't planned, I wanted him. Abortion or adoption never crossed my mind for a second. I did, however, feel very unworthy to be a mom. Given the current state of my life, I knew that something had to change.

That cold February morning, I decided to step into that church doorway. I looked all around for any sign of another person, but it appeared to just be me and God that day. I walked through the doors of the sanctuary and fell on my face crying, "Jesus, help me!" At that moment, I felt the warmth of His presence wrap all around me like a blanket. I felt His love surround me. I laid in His presence for what felt like hours. When I got up off the floor, and walked out of that church, I left a different person than I was when I walked in.

I owe so much to my parents and my sister, Megan, who despite all wounded emotions, were incredibly helpful and supportive to me. They took care of me and prayed for me. I would never have gotten through the pregnancy without them.

I had a very complicated pregnancy. There were still many challenges I was facing in my personal life at the time, and in addition to those stressors, I was attending vocational school full time for Cosmetology. It was a lot. Through all of that, the devil tried to rob me of my son many times. I went into pre-term labor at 14 weeks, 18 weeks, 22 weeks, and 30 weeks. However, during all these difficulties, I kept hearing God say, "I am with you." And I know He was. He was with us both.

At 37 weeks, my water broke. I knew what was happening and that it wasn't something that could be stopped any longer. He was coming early, and there was nothing further I or anyone else could do to stop him.

On the way to the hospital, I sat in the back seat, my dad was driving, and my mom was in the front passenger seat. It was humid and rainy outside. The roads were slippery, and the traffic was heavy. As we stopped at a red light, the car behind us slammed right into the back of our car! I did not have my seatbelt on, so my knees slammed hard into the back of the front seat. My dad was so concentrated on getting me to the hospital that he didn't even care about the car. After making sure the people in the car behind us were okay, he hopped right back in and sped me to the ER of Bridgeton hospital as quickly as possible!

After ten hours of unfruitful labor, I knew something was wrong. I didn't feel right; there was something else going on besides the labor pains. The monitors were showing my baby was in distress. My midwife looked worried; I heard her call in a different doctor and tell him I was preeclamptic. I asked what that meant, and they explained that my blood pressure was so high that

I could have a stroke. I immediately prayed, "Jesus, please help my baby." I remember looking around the room and then suddenly...I blacked out.

Matthew Devon arrived at 10:33pm on September 4th, 2002 via emergency C-section, three weeks before his due date. I don't remember anything about the delivery itself, only waking up in a room with a bright pink baby boy being held in his father's arms. He was beautiful, with silky blonde curls and deep blue eyes (that would later turn into a unique hazel-grey). He was named after his father, Matthew, and my brother, Devon, who passed away. He had a hilarious cry that was very distinctive: "Ah-la-waah!" That was his cry. It was the most beautiful sound I had ever heard.

Hindsight:

When I look back at the story of my first pregnancy, there are things the mind naturally does. I certainly don't look back fondly on the tears and disappointment I caused my parents. Even though they, and my sister, were my greatest support system, they raised me right, and my sin hurt them. I was drunk at a party when I took the pregnancy test, for God's sake! It's true...there are regrets. However, my son has never been one of them. Since the day he arrived, he has been the true earthly hero of my life. In so many ways, he has shown me how to love like I never imagined possible. He has given my life purpose and direction and took me off a path of self-destruction. I truly believe I would be dead if he didn't come to me when he did. He was no accident. I believe he was a gift, hand delivered by God. He was sent with a purpose, just in time to rescue me.

He rescued me from myself.

"Purpose is the divider that separates those who are simply living, from those who are truly alive."
-Alex Rogers

Think about your life situation. Are you where you planned to be, or are you wandering around without purpose? Jesus, who created you with divine purpose, longs to have you come to Him for guidance. Even if you have purposefully started full speed the wrong direction on a one-way street headed for disaster, He is willing, ready, and anxiously awaiting to help you safely back on the right road. Ask for directions. He's got the map! No matter what you are facing, God can turn things around for good. He loves you!

3

My Hope is in You, Lord

"Don't fret or worry. Instead of worrying, pray. Let petitions and praises shape your worries into prayers, letting God know your concerns. Before you know it, a sense of God's wholeness, everything coming together for good, will come settle you down. It is wonderful what happens when Christ displaces worry at the center of your life."
Philippians 4:6-7 (MSG)

NOT THAT THE OB-GYN IS EVER AN EXTREMELY fun place to be, however, I was not only uncomfortable, but excruciatingly nervous. Despite the air conditioning constantly running on the "South Pole" setting in the office that day, I was flushed and sweating, with a pit in my stomach that overwhelmed me. The doctor only left me for a moment; it felt like hours. Every tick the clock made sent little anxiety shocks down my spine.

Since I was a young girl, I had always had a desire to be a mother one day. My heart was so full of love for my son, and my life so much more fulfilled because of him. Matthew (around three at the time) always liked the idea of having a brother or sister in his future. I knew that I wanted more children, and my desire for this never dissipated, even after the horrible news I didn't know I was about to receive.

After the birth of my son, I developed a very painful and life-altering disease called Endometriosis. This is a condition in which scar tissue mutates and attacks your reproductive organs. Once spread, it can attach itself to surrounding areas, such as your intestines, colon, etc. The pain feels as though barbed wire is knotted into your mid-section. It's crippling. I know anyone reading this who has had this disease understands exactly what I'm talking about. It changes your whole life; it absolutely changed mine. There were days that I couldn't move. Eating, walking, and daily activities became a challenge. After a series of doctor's appointments and second opinions, I moved forward with a specialist to see what my options were to control the disease. At first, I wasn't thinking about anything other than the pain. The thought that this could and would affect my ability to conceive any more children, had yet to be explained to me.

My specialist, who is truly one of the kindest and most caring people I have ever met, sat me down and broke the news to me. He had "the face." You know, the face someone makes when they are preparing to give you terrible news. He went on to explain that after my first laparoscopy, they discovered very quickly how serious my condition was. It was so much worse than anyone had anticipated. The scar tissue had spread into my ovaries, the entire lower portion of my uterus, and had already strangled out my right tube. There was also evidence of the disease on my cervix and colon. Even more seriously, it was so widespread it fused my uterus to my intestines.

I don't think I really understood at first, but after it sunk in a little, I asked **the** question, "What does this mean for my future as a mother?" He scooped up my hand, and tried to calm the trembling, as he explained to me that my chances to conceive were extremely unlikely. I think everyone in the building could have audibly heard my heart break.

Anyone who knows me well, knows that I don't go down without a fight. This news, this "you can't," well, I didn't accept that. I moved forward with treatments to do all that I could to fight this disease and fulfill my dream of having more children. Over the course of two years, I underwent four laser scrapings and three different medications. They even gave me a hard-core treatment used to help cancer patients; I lost my hair in chunks as a side effect. But none of that mattered to me...I just wanted to fight!

After all the unsuccessful treatments and surgeries were done, there wasn't anything left to try. I knew then that there was nothing else MAN could do to help me. I could only rely on God to hear the cry of my heart and trust Him and His will for my life.

I was blessed to grow up in a wonderful church and sought out the prayers of a wonderful couple there known for their successful prayers to help women conceive. When my husband (at the time) and I approached the them, they were so gracious. They stood with us, and prayed over my womb, laying their hands on and coming into agreement with us for my healing and for my ability to be a mother again. We thanked the Lord that His Will, no matter what that was, would be done, and that He would give me the strength to accept whatever that would be.

Two weeks later, I found out I was pregnant with my daughter! My doctors could not believe it! They said it was medically impossible for her to have gotten past my tubes. They did not understand that my God was bigger and stronger than any bad report of this world! Nothing is impossible for the Lord, Jesus Christ! It was a miracle...that is why it could not be explained!

This pregnancy was well monitored, as it was considered high risk from all my prior complications. During my eighth week, I tested positive for gestational diabetes and was put on a very strict diet. They would only allow me to gain about 25 pounds, to control both the diabetes and my blood pressure. As you can imagine, for a pregnant woman, not being able to eat anything delicious was torture, but it was totally worth it to ensure my baby girl arrived safely. I fought so hard and so long to have her; if I couldn't have a piece of pie, I would gladly deal with it!

Trinity Hope was born at 10:45am, July 19, 2007, two weeks before her due date. She was a planned C-section, and I was awake for the surgery. I was so nervous. All I wanted to do was hear her cry. I needed to hear her cry. Then suddenly: "QUACK!!!" Quack? Yep, she quacked! Much like her big brother, the Little Miss had her very own unique cry, that made everyone in the delivery room laugh out loud until she settled. She was bright pink like her brother. She was healthy, with a full head of dirty blonde hair and the brightest electric blue eyes I had ever seen. They rushed her to me. She looked so angry, but she was so beautiful! I welled up with tears the second I saw her, kissed her on her little cheek and said, "I've been waiting for you for such a long time!"

Hindsight:

When I look back at the story of my second pregnancy and the hard journey to it, I am overwhelmed by the miracle of my daughter. Yes, there were painful losses, endless tears, great struggles, and heartbreaks along the way, but I know that God didn't allow me to give up hope. He used this difficult journey to strengthen my relationship with Him. He heard the cry and desires of my heart and carried me through to victory. I regret nothing. Sometimes, man can't help us, and that is okay. **BUT GOD!** If His will for you is sought, and it is in sync with the desires of your heart, nothing can stop Him. My daughter is a living miracle. Jesus Christ is the God of miracles.

"For with God nothing shall be impossible."
Luke 1:37 (KJV)

Have you ever, or are you currently, facing what seems to be an impossible situation in your life? Surrender it to Christ. Share your bleeding heart and its desires to Him. Pray for wisdom and strength to accept His answer. This is hard sometimes, because we are afraid the answer might be "no," but we must trust God's perfect will for our lives. He can move mountains for you. Yet, He is also able to give you something different or even better than what you were first wanting. So, trust Him. Put your hope in Him. He loves you.

"Once you choose hope, anything is possible."
-Christopher Reeve

4

Comfort in a Dream

**"I sought the Lord, and he answered me and delivered me
from all of my fears. Those who look to Him are radiant;
and their faces are never covered in shame."
Psalm 34:4-5 (NIV)**

DEAR FRIENDS, I WANT TO SHARE WITH YOU A
dream I had in 2013, two years after the sudden loss of my close
friend, Rory Wilson. The parts that are the dream are in bold.

*I found myself visiting Rory's parents one day, as
I had several times since Rory's passing.*

Visiting them proved to be both comforting and hard.
Comforting, because there is a peace that comes when you surround yourself with people who share your pain, hard because,
well, death is hard.

*I knocked on the door, but this time no one
answered. I took the liberty of letting myself in,*

making my way past the living room, and then stopping dead in my tracks in the dining room.

Rory was standing in the kitchen ten feet from me.

"How is this happening?" I whimpered, while shaking in terror. "You...you're gone. Am I dreaming?" She didn't answer, only smiled her sweet unique underbite of a smile.

To this point, I had been holding it together well, considering one of my best friend's lives had been snuffed out, with no explanation, at such a young age. She just didn't wake up. She was a spirited young woman in her 20's, alive and well before bed, who just didn't wake up. Medical examiners couldn't find a thing wrong with her. She just died. I was, since her passing, trying terribly hard to be a source of strength to those around me who were also suffering this huge, unexplained open wound. I felt overwhelming emotions every day. Some days it was extreme sadness. Some days it was anger. Other days is was both. Still, I had yet to have my moment. You know, the one where you allow yourself to melt into the earth like lava with your pain. That moment. It had not yet arrived.

Rory and I sat on the couch. Mostly, I was just wide eyed in disbelief. "I'm sorry I didn't call you back," I whispered, "I should have called you back."

Two days before Rory died, she called me out of the blue. This wasn't a normal occurrence. Although we met and developed our friendship here in NJ, Rory had long since moved away, and had most recently started a life in Colorado. We communicated often and had tried to have monthly phone dates when we could coordinate them around our busy schedules and time zone differences. Like most people, text and social media were just easier. Phone calls would always be planned. On the Sunday before she died, however, she called me unexpectedly.

I was just getting home from work, had two hyper kids both speaking to me at the same time, and arms full of groceries, when my cell rang. In my flustered state, I wasn't thinking about how weird it was that Rory was randomly calling me. I was so overwhelmed, I just answered and immediately asked if I could call her back. She said it was fine. She sounded fine.

I forgot to call her back.

She died two days later.

This had haunted me with guilt ever since.

> *She didn't say anything back. She laid my head into her lap and I dissolved, letting out everything I had been holding in for so long. I screamed and wailed. She ran her fingers through my hair, kindly and calmingly, until I stopped. She then leaned over and whispered in my ear, "I'm okay, Kate. And you will be too."*

Then...I woke up.

Hindsight:

Looking back, in truth, there will always be a part of me that will feel sorry for not calling my friend back that day. Obviously, if I had known it was the last time I would ever hear her voice, my chosen response would not have been, "I'll have to call you back." Regret. We all have it in some way. This experience of loss allowed me to learn how precious every moment is, and how to treat every second you have with someone as if it were your last. More importantly, I believe the Lord, in His great kindness and comfort, gave me the dream as a message of peace and as an outlet to have my much-needed breakdown. How incredible. He allowed me to have it in the arms of the very friend I was mourning. God sometimes comforts us in the most unexpected ways.

"If your heart is broken, you'll find God right there; if you're kicked in the gut, he'll help you catch your breath."
Psalm 34:18 (MSG)

I cannot begin to know what pain or regrets you might carry. All I know is that I promise you, you are never alone. Jesus Christ loves you with an everlasting love, and He wants to heal you everywhere you hurt. Through Him, you gain inner peace and strength to face the challenges and losses in this life. Without Him, we are hopeless, but with Him, we have hope and healing. Have you given Him your pain? Let Him carry you; life is too painful to limp through alone. He loves you.

5

A Legacy of Love

> "Love leaves legacy. How you treated other people, not
> your wealth or accomplishments, is the most enduring
> impact you can leave on earth."
> -Pastor Rick Warren

THE TRAGEDY OF LIFE, IT OFTEN SEEMS, IS WHEN A person of extreme talent and worth, has a brief life. After losing my friend Rory in October of 2011, my heart was still bleeding. I had never lost a close personal friend like that before, and I knew that I didn't want to suffer another loss like that again. But life… well, part of life is death. I just didn't realize it was going to strike me so hard a second time in less than a year.

Ted walked into the sanctuary doors of the church I grew up in, with his family for the first time in 1999. I was drawn to him and his stepbrother, Dan, immediately. They had a similar style and shared the same teenage angst I did. We became fast friends.

He looked like a real-life version of Trent Lane from the MTV cartoon series *Daria* (Google it). That is the best way I can describe him! I mean, take out Trent's earrings, and you have Ted! He was a musician, beach bum, singer, jokester, cigarette enthusiast, and royal pain!

We had a lot of fun, Ted and I. The kind that probably annoyed other people! Like, going to the boardwalk and getting free samples from Steel's Fudge, then walking around the corner, switching around our clothes and going back for more! We would do this repeatedly, until they would catch on, cut us off, and make us leave! We wanted to see how long it would take for them to crack! That was us, a couple of silly kids. I will forever cherish every ridiculous moment we shared.

The memory of Ted, and the one I hold dearest to my heart, is when for a period in 2003, I was living alone in an apartment with my son. Things in my life were not good. In fact, I wasn't sure where my life was even going at that point. By that time, I had not seen Ted in person for at least a year. To this day, I have no idea how he even got my address. Nevertheless, one day I got a knock at the door. I opened it, and there he was, standing there with a goofy look on his face. I was so surprised; I didn't even know what to say.

"Hey," he said, in his quick way. "What are you doing here?" I replied, with tears already filling my eyes. He went on to say that he had heard about the challenges I was facing, and he had to find me. I was scared to let him in. Scared because I couldn't hide from Ted, you know? He could see right through me, and I didn't want to be vulnerable. What was happening in my life at the time was so hard and so painful. I needed to keep it together. I had to be strong for my son. I didn't want to fall apart. Numb was safe. Numb was what I wanted.

I came out to him instead, and we sat on a bench on my outside terrace. I wouldn't make eye contact with him. He knew what I was doing, and he called me out on it. "Woman!" he shouted, "Look at me, Kate. Look at me." He grabbed my chin, turned my head toward him, and forced my forehead onto his, holding it there, no matter how hard I tried to pull away. At that moment, it all came out. Not words, just tears. All the emotions and pain I had been holding in, came flooding out, and they flowed until there were none left. He never let me go. The snot and makeup running down my face never mattered to him; he just held me there until I was done. It was exactly what I needed, and he knew that because he knew me. This is what made him so special. He knew how to love me. He knew how to be my friend.

He came in for a minute and looked into my sleeping son's crib. "He is beautiful. You don't deserve tears, Kate, you deserve joy. Find happiness," he said softly. I walked him to his car, where we shared a hug I never wanted to end. That was the last time I would see him in person again.

In April of 2012, Ted called me out of the blue. I remember immediately thinking something was wrong. He said he was fine but was talking with a different tone than usual. He started saying some things that concerned me; not what would normally concern a regular person. See, Ted and I joked…all of the time. We were snarky and sarcastic in our banter. It's who we were. I say, "What's up, jerk?", and he would reply something like, "Nothing… still ugly. You?" That was the norm for us, but that day…that call, he was overly serious and super sweet. It felt like a goodbye. I listened, confused and concerned. I told him he was scaring me. He was quiet. I was nauseous. Eventually, he replied, "Kate…don't be scared. I just wanted to tell you that I love you and am grateful for everything you have been to me over the years. It is important to me that you know that."

After that, I decided to just shut up and listen. When he was done sharing his heart, I decided to do the same. I told him everything there was to possibly say. I didn't want to lose this moment. I thanked him for his ridiculous jokes, his songs, his transparency, and his friendship. I reminded him how proud I was of him and that I treasured his heart. I reminded him of how much he mattered and how grateful I was that God gifted us to each other. It was a long, emotionally draining conversation, that I will forever be grateful for.

Two months later, Ted passed away suddenly of a heart related issue at the age of 29 years old. He was a treasure. He mattered.

Hindsight:

The friendship I had with Ted, truly was a gift from God. Although his time on earth was not long, his love and kindness changed my life. He is missed with sorrow, but celebrated with pride, as a person who spoke life into my broken heart and who gave encouragement in some of my darkest hours. He was flawed, but he had a beautiful heart. What an amazing legacy to leave behind. I pray that from Heaven he can still feel and know that people smile from ear to ear when they think of him.

"A new command I give you: Love one another. As I have loved you, so you must love one another. By this everyone will know that you are my disciples, if you love one another." John 13:34-35 (NIV)

Have you ever wondered what others would remember about you? What type of legacy do you think you would be leaving behind if today was your last? Allow the answers, or lack of answers, to help you self-examine. Ask the Lord to help you live each day in a way that is not only pleasing to Him, but in a way that would point others to Him with your love. If you need to make changes, that's okay. Ask Jesus for forgiveness, guidance and a deep compassion for others. Love changes lives. Let love be your legacy.

6

The Impossible

"Nothing is impossible, the word itself says, "I'm possible!"
-Audrey Hepburn

WHEN I WAS AROUND SEVEN OR EIGHT YEARS OLD, my parents brought me over to the home of Dave and Christine Strittmatter, close friends of theirs, to have dinner. I enjoyed going over because they had children to play with. Their son, Sam, was closest to my age.

Sam and I decided to ride bikes around the property. Sam, of course, knew the twists and turns of the yard, driveway, and paths much better than I did. I was competitive though, and could not resist a good bike race, even if it ended in my demise. This time it did…big time. We were riding fast down a dirt path, and I turned my bike too late and too sharply, sliding myself right into a brick wall.

Initially, I felt nothing. I couldn't get up though. I was dazed and confused, although I didn't hit my head. I saw Sam run into the house and all four adults run back out. Finally, I looked down and saw it…the bone. A sharp, jagged bone piercing through the flesh of my leg, just below my knee. I could see blood pouring down, puddling under me. I almost passed out from the sight of it. The eyes of the adults were all enlarged. They managed to remain calm, but I can't imagine the actual horror they must have been feeling.

The grownups surrounded me; my father and Mr. Strittmatter knelt beside me. They took their hands and hovered them over my wound. Then they prayed out loud, asking the Lord to help and heal me.

When they were done praying, they lifted their hands away and it was gone. I mean, really gone. The bone was back inside of my leg, the skin was healed over, and the blood had literally disappeared. The exit wound that the bone had been sticking out of was scarred over.

The adults all looked at each other with both shock and excitement, giving thanks to the Lord for the miracle He performed. I got up and continued to play as if nothing had happened to me at all.

It was impossible.

But God.

Hindsight:

No one can ever tell me that God isn't real. I have seen the proof, not just with this one experience, but in many. When I think back on that day, or when I look down at my leg, I smile in constant awe and wonder at the impossible things our amazing God can do!

"And these signs will accompany those who believe…they will place their hands on sick people, and they will get well."
Mark 16:17-18 (NIV)

Remember, friends, that the same power that raised Christ from the dead, dwells in you. You have the ability, through Jesus, to speak healing over yourself and those around you, and if it is in line with the perfect will of God, miracles can happen. He is the God of miracles! He makes the impossible possible!

7

The Joy of Friendship

**"Because of you, I laugh a little harder, cry a little less,
and smile a lot more."**
(Unknown)

"MARC," I WHISPERED, "WATCH THE STAIRS!"

"Yo! Hurry up!" he whispered with nervous laughter.

The game was Drop and Roll, a very mature and not at all dangerous activity we four high school seniors would play while our teachers would be with the other students at lunch time. Rachel, Jenn, and I got in a line. Marc kept watch. The mission? To run down our school hallway as fast as humanly possible, one after the other, five seconds apart–each of us having to launch ourselves like Superman onto the couch at the end of the hall and roll off onto the floor before the next person landed. This may or may not have resulted in injury on occasion, but it was totally worth it! The holes in the drywall behind the couch must have gotten there on their own. We surely had nothing to do with it.

Rachel and I were born one day apart, so we only knew life with each other in it. Jenn and Marc joined our school junior year. We were all so different, but we gravitated to each other, forming a lifetime bond filled with memories of joy and laughter. We fell together like a beautiful mess. Rachel was loud, Jenn was sarcastic, Marc was hilarious, and I was crazy. We drove our teachers insane. I'm sure they were ready for us to graduate and stop torturing them, but I am forever grateful for that little private school 'in the middle of nowhere.' It brought these three mischievous, genuine people into my life and heart, and I am forever changed because of it.

Twenty years later, we are all still connected, loving and supporting each other through life and all its twist and turns. I don't know what I would do without them. They are forever a part of me.

Hindsight:

What's the great lesson in this little story, right? For me, it is the appreciation of the simple joys of friendship.

The journey of life is more bearable when we have friends with which to share the highs and lows. Friends are your chosen family. To look back and have cherished memories with loving individuals who chose me, brings a joy like no other.

"The sweet smell of incense can make you feel good,
but true friendship is better still."
Proverbs 27:9 (CEV)

God takes great pleasure in friendship. He knows that the world we live in is painful and full of sorrow. He created man for fellowship, so that we can support and love each other through it. Just as He longs to have relationship with us, He knew we would need other people to relate to. I believe that He truly created some people specifically with others in mind. When the paths of people destined for each other cross, God smiles, because He finds joy in the happiness friendship can bring. Thank Him for the good people He has placed in your life.

8

God Knows Best

"Instead of your shame, you will have a double portion, and instead of humiliation, they will shout for joy over their portion. Therefore, they will possess a double portion in their land. Everlasting joy will be theirs."
Isaiah 61:7 (MEV)

DREAM FROM THE LORD – 2012

I was in a cold, dirty basement. It was full of old boxes filled with junk. I was frantically searching for something; I felt the stress and urgency. I felt the panic and desperation.

"I can't find it!" I repeated several times, with tears streaming down my face. I tore the whole room apart, going through every box several times.

Then I heard a voice yelling from the top of the stairs.

"What are you looking for?" it asked.

"My gift!!" I explained. "I have to find it!!"

"You have to let it go," the voice gently replied.

I didn't accept this answer. I wanted this thing I was looking for, even though I didn't even really know what it was. I opened the Bilco doors exiting the basement and ran outside. I saw him there (my ex). He was holding a clumsily wrapped present. It was tattered and torn.

He began taunting me with it.

"Looking for this?!" he snickered.

He turned and started running away from me. I chased him, but I could never catch up.

(It was so real, that I felt the sweat running down my face).

Suddenly, a large angel appeared. It rushed between us. My ex dropped the box at the angel's feet and ran away.

Now, my gift is right in front of me, but before I can reach down to grab it, the angel crushed it underneath his feet.

"Why did you do that?!" I reprimanded.

"It is what you want; it is not what you need," the angel replied calmly.

The angel reached behind its back and pulled out two beautifully wrapped gifts. They were shiny and perfect, gold and silver, and warm to the touch.

"If you stop chasing what was never really meant for you, God will bring you a double portion of blessing to replace what you have lost. He will restore. Trust Him," it ended with reassuring kindness.

Hindsight:

The Lord was showing me how unhealthy it was for me to hold on to the past. I was to let those things GO, and trust God to restore my joy with whatever HE had planned for me. See, to me, my greatest gift in life, is my children. My deepest sadness, back then, was that I couldn't have any more. In 2010, my endometriosis had become so bad, I had to finally go ahead and have a full hysterectomy. That was the only way to rid myself of the disease for good. So, with my baby box gone, I resolved in my heart to be grateful beyond words for my two amazing children. I knew that many women often long to even have ONE child, so I knew how incredibly blessed I already was. However, there is something very unsettling and intimidating about having a surgery that was so permanent and final, regardless of what you do or don't already have. I knew that the Lord was telling me through this dream, that I needed to surrender my losses to Him, and TRUST Him with my future.

In 2013, I met my husband…and my TWO amazing stepchildren. My double portion. The Lord filled my void to overflowing! He gave me the big family I had always dreamed of having. All I had to do was trust Him.

> **"Trust in the Lord with all your heart; and lean
> not onto your own understanding. In all thy ways
> acknowledge him, and he shall direct your paths."
> Proverbs 3:5-6 (KJV)**

How often do you do that? Try to control your own life.

Do you find yourself still desperately holding onto the past, or allowing the pain and disappointments of it to control your actions and rob you of your peace? I think we all have been guilty of this in some way. The lives we build for ourselves got turned upside down somehow, and we are desperate to fix it ourselves, or to hold onto it, when the Lord is gently trying to pull us forward into the new things He has for us. But we are humans. Let's face it, we have MAJOR trust issues. So, we often battle ourselves and the Lord through these transitions.

The bottom line is this: holding onto the past leaves us in limbo. It paralyzes us, and that is just what the devil wants. Surrendering our hurts, disappointments, and future to the Lord is the ultimate act of trust…and His promises are true. He is faithful. Trust Him. He loves you.

> **"Every difficulty you face, in every waiting place,
> you're being given the chance to trust in the things
> unseen and to be abundantly blessed."**
> -Cherie Hill

9

Beauty from Ashes

"Behind every beautiful thing, there is some kind of pain."
-Bob Dylan

IN THE PAST, I HAVE FELT USED, BETRAYED, AND
beaten down. I dealt with may hardships and deep inner wounds
for most of my young adult life. I have struggled with insecurity,
depression, and feeling insignificant. People have hurt me deeply.
People I loved.

The Lord has often pointed me to the story of Cinderella. After
her father died, she was no longer treasured and valued, but instead
rejected and abused. She was treated poorly in her own home by
the people who were supposed to love and take care of her. Not
only was she constantly belittled, she had to stay and serve the
people mistreating her. She longed to feel a part of the family and
tried everything she could to get them to love her. Yet, the more she
would try, the more they would despise her. It was never enough.
They left her in rags and emotionally stripped her of all her dignity.
She felt alone and devastated by their actions.

Later in the story though, we find that all that was taken from
her and done to her turned out to be for the preparation of the

fulfillment of her dreams. The ill treatment she endured prepared and equipped her for her great destiny.

Imprisoned and abandoned, she cried out for help, and along came her fairy godmother to the rescue! Cinderella was set free, renewed, clothed with riches, and arrived at the ball with confidence. Even though she still had some challenges, by the end of her story she was loved, restored, and crowned as royalty.

Hindsight:

In my life, there have been people I loved that didn't love me back the way they should have, and it wounded my soul. It made me feel like I didn't matter. Amid my moments of desperation, Jesus has always been faithful to reveal Himself to me when I would call on Him, assuring me to trust Him with my future. Without fail, each time I have put my trust in Him, He has faithfully restored and healed me. More importantly, He has used the pain and hardships I have endured, to help me be able to empathize with others and point them to Him.

"Consider it pure joy, my brothers and sisters, whenever you face trials of many kinds, because you know that the testing of your faith produces perseverance. Let the perseverance finish its work so that you may be mature and complete, not lacking anything."
James 1:2-4 (NIV)

Indeed, through all your trials, you are being prepared for your destiny in Jesus Christ. You are truly loved by your heavenly Father and are resting in the palm of His hand. Your life belongs to Him, and He will see that you receive the untold blessings He's kept in waiting for you. Cry out to Him amid your troubles and in the moments that you doubt your value! You are His beloved and favored child–His special creation. Find your confidence in Him! He loved you enough to die for you; that's how valuable He thinks you are!

He makes beauty from the ashes of our lives.

10

You are God's Hands

"When Jesus came down from the mountainside, large
crowds followed him. A man with leprosy came and
knelt before Him and said, "Lord, if you are willing,
you can make me clean." Jesus reached out his hand
and touched the man. "I am willing," he said. "Be
clean!" Immediately he was cleansed of his leprosy."
Matthew 8:1-3 (NIV)

IN 2010, THE CHURCH I WAS ATTENDING FOCUSED
on the story of Jesus and the leper for a few Sundays in a row. I was
deeply touched by the study. The story itself has always brought
me to tears. The love of Christ for us as individuals is so beautiful
and challenges us to reflect that to others.

Back in those days, someone with leprosy was abandoned and
rejected. They were told and believed that they were cursed by
God. They were considered unclean and totally outcast. The sickness could not be hidden; they literally wore it on their face. They
were required by law to stay far away from everyone. If someone
approached them, they had to identify themselves by yelling
"unclean" aloud, so people could go the other way.

This leper, despite the rules, was bold and approached Jesus. He declared his faith in what Jesus could do for him. He did not demand Christ to heal him, he asked Him if He would be willing. Basically saying, "Jesus, I know what I am; I am unclean, and unworthy, but I know who You are, and I know if you are willing, You can heal me."

Hindsight:

There have been many times in my personal life that I remember feeling so unworthy of God's love and help. But I can tell you that in my darkest hours, with all my brokenness, He reached out and grabbed me when I needed Him the most. He healed me everywhere I hurt, inside and out. He was just waiting for me to ask Him and trust Him.

> **"For even if the mountains walk away and the hills**
> **fall to pieces, my love won't walk away from you. My**
> **covenant commitment of peace won't fall apart.**
> **The God who has compassion says so."**
> **Isaiah 54:10 (MSG)**

God cares deeply about our inner pain, insecurities, voids, and scars. It would have been easy for Jesus to just wave His hand and heal the leper like a magician, but, no, He reached out and laid His hands on him. He realized the man's feelings of abandonment and lack of human contact were just as important to heal as the disease. That is what Jesus wants to do for you. He wants to give you strength and use His power to change your life; He wants to heal you inside and out.

The leper was not part of the great crowd; he was on the outskirts. Jesus and the leper had to make their way to each other. And

He does that, doesn't He? He meets us exactly where we are. Our circumstances don't matter; when we ask for help, He makes His way to us, where we are and as we are. He doesn't care what our dirt is. Jesus makes the unclean clean! His compassion is without limit.

11

Not Alone

**"A friend loves at all times, and a brother (or sister)
is born for a time of adversity."
Proverbs 17:17 (NIV)**

I WANTED TO SHARE ABOUT A SPECIFIC SMALL group of friends in my life that I refer to as "my crew." We are like a family...a chosen family. I'm going to tell you a little about four of them...specifically about their character.

Charissa

Charissa has this magnetism, this shimmering light that surrounds her. I'm certain that it's the light of God. She has a calling on her life to just wake up and make the people around her better for sharing time and space with her. She loves people the way they need to be loved, at their best and worst. She is loyal, compassionate, and giving. She is honest, even when you don't want to hear the truth. She is genuine and real. She never plays games with anyone's heart or mind. She challenges people to be the best version of themselves. Like Jesus, who can look past the mess and see who we were meant to be, she loves without condition.

Dori

Dori is an overwhelming example of strength and courage. She has a bleeding heart that belongs fully to Jesus and to those she loves. Like Christ, Dori is faithful to come running any time someone needs her. She brings joy and heartfelt laughter everywhere she goes.

Ricky

Being the court jester of our group, Ricky can always be counted on to say and do the most ridiculous things. An overcomer of much, he has always had faith in the Lord and exhibited gratitude for the things and people in his life. God gave him the heart of a peacemaker. He is dedicated and loyal to anyone and everyone he considers family or friend.

Jodi

Jodi is one of the strongest women I know. Life isn't fair to any of us, but the way Jodi has chosen to carry herself through this unfair life has always been an inspiration to me. God uses her to bless others with her thoughtfulness and servant's heart. She is always willing to offer a helping hand, a sarcastic comment, or a warm embrace...whatever you may need at the time.

"Friends are the family you choose."
-Jess C. Scott

The story I am about to share with you is difficult. There was another member of our group, her name was Aimee. She was a spitfire. Little, but fierce. She was an absolute joy to know, and we all loved her. We miss her. We miss her because we lost her.

In the winter of 2016, I received a phone call that shook my world. Death was coming to steal our Aimee. I remember my state of disbelief. It was so surreal; I kept forgetting to breathe. I sat on my bedroom floor with my head between my knees saying, "This isn't happening," repeatedly.

A short while later, Charissa, Dori, Ricky, Jodi, and I took what felt like the longest drive of my life. We headed to the hospital to say goodbye. I don't even know if we spoke on that car ride; I can't remember. This wasn't supposed to be something we were actually about to do. I still find it hard to believe that we lived through it at all…or survived it, I should say.

Many things happened that day at the hospital. It was a day filled with shock, agony, disbelief, and heartbreak. However, that day I felt the Lord answering my prayers through my friends. I was filled with the overwhelming re-realization that the four people God had with me there that day, were four of the greatest human beings on planet earth. I understood how truly blessed and divinely favored I was to have them as a support system. We cried together. We held each other. We took walks together. We sat silently together. We prayed together. They made me feel safe.

We said goodbye to our precious Aimee that day as both friends and family. God was looking out for all of us and provided what we needed in one of our darkest hours. We got through it because God gave us each other.

Hindsight:

I think that is the most important thing you can do for someone else: make them feel safe in your love. Just as my friends were there for me that day, God had me in place to be there for them as well. Strength, courage, and comfort can be found in Godly friendship. Additionally, and most importantly, I realize that I didn't have four friends with me there that day...I had five. I had Jesus.

"One who has unreliable friends soon comes to ruin, but there is a friend that sticks closer than a brother."
Proverbs 18:24 (NIV)

God tells us to "do unto others as we would have them do to us" (Luke 6:36). We should always strive to be the type of friend we would want to have. I don't know how my friends would describe me, but my sincere hope is that at the very least, they would say they know I love them. Jesus is remembered for His love and compassion. Our relationship with Him gives us a feeling of safety, like no other. Let's strive to be like Him in the lives of the ones we love.

12

Inner Peace

"Do not be anxious about anything, but in every situation, by prayer and petition, with thanksgiving, present your request to God. And the peace of God, which transcends all understanding, will guard your hearts and your minds in Christ Jesus."
Philippians 4:6-7 (NIV)

IN 2018, MY FOUR CHILDREN AND I VISITED MY parent's church to hear a special guest speaker that was going to be preaching that Sunday. He is well known and drew in a large crowd of guests to the church that morning. We were among them, and very much looking forward to hearing him speak.

We arrived at the second service, just as the first service was being dismissed. We made our way past the exiting crowd and found our seats that my mother had saved at the front row. It was brought to my attention by a friend, that during first service a "fan" of the speaker had rushed the stage at him and had to be stopped by security. I didn't think much of it, as everyone there currently looked happy and peaceful.

There were still a few minutes before the second service began, so we were chit-chatting with the people around us. My mother, sister, and niece made their way over to sit with us, but my father had attended the first service. He came over to say a quick "hi and goodbye," making his way out of the back doors to head home.

Suddenly, we heard screams coming from the same direction my father had exited toward the back of the church! Two security members came in and yelled, "GET DOWN!" and held their backs against the doors. Before I could even react, I looked over to my children, who had obeyed orders before they were even done being spoken. Three of them were tucked under the church pews, and my oldest, who is bigger than I am, was down on the ground with his hands over his head. I immediately threw my body over him, creating a shield the best I could.

My blood ran cold as I heard someone shout, "GUN!" I looked around, finding my mother lying on the ground nearby. My three youngest were still tucked tearfully under their seats. I heard my youngest son, Christian, praying in tongues as quietly as possible. I turned my head to the right, to find my sister shielding my niece the same way I was stacked over my oldest son.

The room was full of families and seniors. Everyone's face was wearing a different shade of terror. Everyone was praying and holding onto each other. It felt like a bad dream.

As the yelling from outside continued, I suddenly remembered my father had gone out those doors only seconds before the drama began. I looked over to my sister, and tearfully whimpered, "Daddy..."

I quietly called out to God, "Help us, Jesus!" and a supernatural calm came over me. I realized fully and clearly, in that moment, that no matter what was about to happen, we were going to be okay. My parents, my sister, my niece, my children...we were all saved. We all had chosen to give our heart and spirits to the Lord, so I knew where each of us were going if something bad were to happen. A peace that passes all understanding just flooded over me, and all fear left. I began to just repeatedly say, "Thank you, Jesus."

Moments later, someone came in and gave the all clear.

Out in the parking lot, the same man who had rushed the stage during first service, had apparently attacked the security guard who had stopped him. He had made threatening remarks that led to the panic and lockdown. Multiple people, including my father, were finally able to subdue him. There were only minor injuries, and we all walked away that day, shook up, but fine.

Hindsight:

When I look back on that day, I feel so blessed. That sounds crazy, I know, but it is true. It truly developed an even deeper level of relationship with the Lord for me. To have trust and peace when knowing it was possible for me or loved ones to die, is truly a peace that passes all understanding. I knew no matter what happened, we were all going to be okay. This life is temporary; eternal life in Heaven awaits all those who believe. What an overwhelming hope that knowledge brings.

"Let the peace of Christ rule in your hearts, since as members of one body you were called to peace. And be thankful."
Colossians 3:15 (NIV)

As a follower of Christ, you can have peace through whatever situations this temporary life brings.

I encourage you to share the Good News of Jesus and the gift of eternal life He offers, with all those you love. It will change your thinking from earthly to eternal. And when you see through eternity-based eyes, your heart will find peace during storms, joy during trial, trust during hardship, and faith through anything that comes your way.

Jesus brings peace.

"Peace. It does not mean to be in a place where there is no noise, trouble or hard work. It means to be in the midst of those things and still be calm in your heart."
(Unknown)

13

Made to Be Different

"In the end, only kindness matters."
-Jewel

In 2015, I met Eleanor. She was 60 years old, but in every emotional way, a child. Riddled with addiction and mental health issues, she battled through life, often losing more than winning. She had a broken heart and a shattered life, yet, she was still kind and still gentle. She needed and wanted to be loved—loved in a way she had yet to experience.

Despite her issues, with wisdom always in place, my husband, children, and I were instructed by the Lord to develop a relationship with Eleanor. We made this love unconditional. We made this love shown. There were periods of time that the children could not be a part of the time spent with her, specifically when she would be active in her addictions, but during those times, they prayed for her relentlessly and faithfully. I was so impressed and in awe of the compassion in their hearts for this broken individual. I was inspired by their kindness and goodness.

One day, Eleanor agreed to join our family for church. She had a prior conversation with my husband, stating that she saw something very different about our children that she couldn't figure out. Matt (my husband) explained to her that they had Jesus in their hearts, and that was what made them different. With tears, she said to him, "I want what they have."

At the time, we were attending Life Church in Williamstown, N.J., pastored by Dr. Rev. Jamie Morgan (a church body filled with wonderful people, and a Pastor who unapologetically speaks truth in love. We forever hold them dear to our hearts). That day, Pastor Jamie spoke powerfully on God's unconditional love and His desire to own your heart and change your life. After service, Eleanor approached the pastor and asked her to lead her into giving her heart to the Lord. It was a beautiful day.

After that day, our relationship with Eleanor grew into something very strong and joyful. Frequent visits and holidays were even shared, much like real families would. The children adored her, and she lit up every time they were with her.

Sadly, there were still many trials and hard times that arose, when her addictions would resurface and get the best of her. We believe her life ended early because of it. We lost her very suddenly in the spring of 2019. Our hearts were broken, but our spirits were peaceful. The children were devastated when Matt and I told them, but we took the opportunity to share with them how through their love, kindness, and Christ-like example, Eleanor was inspired to give God and church a chance. She told us she saw something special and different about them, and that she wanted that for herself. The seeds they sowed, just by being themselves, led her to her Salvation. They smiled through their tears at the knowledge that they made a difference in someone's life. As a family, it was normal for us to be sad that we lost her, but we were grateful for now knowing we will see her again one day in Heaven.

Hindsight:

This experience has shown our children how deeply kindness matters, how it can literally change someone's eternal destiny. Eleanor mattered. She just needed someone to tell her and to show her. She was searching for something, and in the kindness of children, she found Jesus.

"Therefore if you have any encouragement from being united with Christ, if any comfort from his love, if any common sharing in the Spirit, if any tenderness and compassion, then make my joy complete by being like-minded, having the same love, being one in spirit and of one mind. Do nothing out of selfish ambition or vain conceit. Rather, in humility value others above yourselves, not looking to your own interests but each of you to the interests of others. In your relationships with one another, have the same mindset as Christ Jesus."
Philippians 2:1-5 (NIV)

We have but one job in this life–to be a living, breathing example of Christ's love to a broken world. How else will they know who Jesus is, if we don't show them?

Stay eternally focused, as you live your daily life, and interact with the lost souls that surround you. Be that very "different" person in their lives that leads them to ask what is it you have that they don't. You can introduce them to the answer: Jesus.

"Do things for people, not because of who they are or what they do in return, but because of who you are."
-Harold S. Kushner

14

Arms Wide Open

**"...But while he was still a long way off, his father saw him
and was filled with compassion for him; he ran to his son,
threw his arms around him and kissed him."
Luke 15:20 (NIV)**

I WAS FORTUNATE ENOUGH, THROUGH THE HARD
work and sacrifices of my parents, to attend a small private
Christian school from K-12. The school was an extension of an
Assemblies of God church called Fairton Christian Center, pastored by Rev. Woodson Moore and his wife Shirley.

Every day I was taught the truth. Every day God's Word was
implanted deep down in my heart. Like many kids, however, I
often challenged and ignored many of the lessons gifted to me. I
grew up and rebelled. I did things my way instead of God's way.

As you can already guess, as the Word of God promises, there
were consequences to my sins. I lost much. I hurt many. I broke
my own heart...all because I wanted to do things my way. By 19, I
was pregnant and unwed.

That year, Mrs. Moore's father, Joe Bennett, passed away suddenly. He was a beloved teacher at the school while I was growing

up, and I loved him. I was so sad that he had passed, and I really wanted to attend his funeral. I was nervous though. Ashamed. I knew that Pastor Moore would see I was pregnant, and I thought about how disappointed he was going to be in me, after teaching me better than that for over 13 years. I struggled with the fear of attending, but in the end, I decided to go.

When I entered the building, my heart was beating fast with anxiety. I struggled to even look up at anyone, not knowing what was going to be said or thought. Suddenly I heard Pastor Moore's voice shout, "Katy-Mae!" I looked up and saw him running toward me, arms wide open. He rushed to me, threw his arms around me, and kissed me on the top of my head. He placed his hand on my belly, and said, "I love you."

Hindsight:

This moment of mercy and unconditional love meant so much to me. Pastor Moore literally WAS Jesus at that moment, showing me undeserved acceptance and forgiveness, loving me despite my sins, and running to me with JOY when I felt unworthy. You can't be more like Jesus than that. I will never forget how that example of Christ's love touched my heart. I will never forget the vision of Pastor Moore's open arms running toward me, like the father running to his prodigal son.

"…God is love. Whoever lives in love lives in God, and God in them."
1 John 4:16b (NIV)

Jesus told the story of the prodigal son to make a point: nevermind what you've done, just come home. No matter how far we wander, He will always run to welcome us back. That is how He loves us; that is how we are to love each other. We all go off course in our lives, taking paths that were clearly the wrong direction. Just as God Almighty forgives us and continues to love us, that mercy is within each of us to also give…with arms wide open.

15

Breakthrough

"But verily God hath heard me; he hath attended
to the voice of my prayer."
Psalm 66:19 (KJV)

MY OLDEST SON MATTHEW WAS DIAGNOSED WITH
Asperger's syndrome (which is a mild form of autism) at three
years old. I've often wondered how deeply he felt the things I would
teach him about Jesus, because he is a very <u>tangible</u> and literal
person. It makes faith a hard concept for him sometimes.

When he was 14 years old, we went to a praise service at
Chestnut Assembly of God in Vineland, New Jersey. They asked
anyone who wanted special prayer for a miracle or breakthrough
to come up and receive prayer, so I went. I asked for prayer for
several things, which will remain private, but one of those things
was for there to be a breakthrough in my son's true understanding
of God, and that the Lord would reveal Himself to Matthew in a
way only He knew he specifically needed.

The worship service was amazing and anointed. I just spent a
lot of time praying in the Spirit over Matthew, releasing my burden

of worry to the Lord. As worship ended, Matthew came over to me and said,

> *"Mom, during the singing we did, I felt amazing and like my heart grew! Like, how it must feel when God touches your heart. I think I <u>felt</u> Him! Do you think He touched my heart?! I never <u>felt</u> anything like that before!"*

Astonished, I replied,

> *"Yes, baby. I think He must have! See, we don't worship Jesus for us, we worship Him to bless Him and let Him know we love him..."*

Matthew interrupts –

> *"So, because I blessed Him by worshiping, He blessed me by letting me feel Him?!"*

Tearfully, I reply,

> *"Yes, baby. That's right."*

Matthew (with the world's biggest smile) whispers,

> *"I really like that feeling."*

Hindsight:

God knew that my son literally needed to FEEL Him and answered my prayers by specifically giving Matthew the actual sensation of his heart being touched. It was a miracle and testimony of God's attention to detail. It did not just grow my son in faith, it grew me.

"If ye shall ask anything in my name, I will do it."
John 14:14 (KJV)

Do you trust God with the seemingly impossible? Are you limiting what He can do? He is a God of miracles. He cares for you, and He loves you. How far are you willing to stretch your faith? Miracles are not only His job; you have to take part in it by asking and trusting.

16

The Condition of Your Heart

"If I speak in the tongues of men or of angels, but have not
love (for others growing out of God's love for me), then I
have become only a noisy gong or a clanging cymbal (just
an annoying distraction). If I have the gift of prophecy (and
speak a new message from God to the people), and can understand all mysteries, and (possess) all knowledge; and if I have
(sufficient) faith so that I can remove mountains, but I do not
love (reaching out to others), I am nothing. If I give all my
possessions to feed the poor, and surrender my body to be
burned, but I do not have love, it does me no good at all."
1 Corinthians 13:1-3 (AMP)

WHEN I WAS IN SCHOOL, THERE WAS A GRUMPY OLD
man named Mr. Levy who used to teach piano lessons. He was
friendly with our superintendent, and hung out at the school a lot,
even when he was not teaching. Most kids feared him because of
his hard disposition.

One day, I overheard him talking to another teacher about
how "most of these kids couldn't memorize anything larger than
a single verse from the Bible." I, being an ornery teen, interjected

quite confidently, "I could!" He looked at me like I had three heads. He raised his eyebrows and looked at me with doubt. Then he sarcastically dared me to prove it.

I accepted the challenge and the terms:

1) *Memorize the entire book of Jonah beginning to end.*
2) *No more than three helps.*
3) *Recite it in front of the entire school at Friday assembly the following week.*

The prize:
$100

Easiest money I ever made. Mr. Levy was both shocked and annoyed. He *did,* however, honor his word, and gave me both the money and an apology for the doubt he had displayed.

Hindsight:

Little did I know before this challenge, the true impact the memorization of this Biblical passage would have on my life moving forward.

The Lord's desire to save the people of Nineveh shows His constant desire to show mercy to the lost. He gives us all so many chances and desires desperately to save us. How much more could He prove it later, when He sacrificed His own Son? What a loving God.

"Do I take any pleasure in the death of the wicked?"
declares the Sovereign Lord. "Rather, am I not pleased
when they turn from their ways and live?"
Ezekiel 18:23 (NIV)

I remember how unsettled I felt about Jonah's attitude. He bothered me. I see now that it was actually the condition of his heart that troubled me. See, Jonah was a believer. He loved the Lord and had a relationship with Him, but when the Lord asked Jonah to go warn the lost people of Nineveh to change their ways, so they could be saved, Jonah didn't want to do it.

He didn't want them to be saved. He felt they deserved to be destroyed and didn't like that the Lord wanted to offer them repentance and mercy. How ugly is that?

> **"God saw what they did and that they had turned from
> their evil lives. He did change his mind about them.
> What he said he would do to them, he didn't do.
> Jonah was furious. He lost his temper. He yelled at God,
> "God! I knew it – when I was back home, I knew this was
> going to happen! That is why I ran off to Tarshish! I knew
> you were sheer grace and mercy, not easily angered, rich
> in love, and ready at the drop of a hat to turn your plans of
> punishment into a program of forgiveness!
> So, God, if you won't kill them, kill me! I'm better off dead.
> God said, "What do you have to be angry about?"
> But Jonah just left. He went out of the city to the
> eat and sat down in a sulk..."**
> **Jonah 3:10 – 4:5a (MSG)**

Yet, when his own sin and disobedience found him cast out to sea and in the belly of a fish, Jonah cried out to the Lord to forgive and save him. Hypocritical, huh? He, who knew the Lord, had no forgiveness, grace, compassion, or love to offer anyone else. For that reason, Jonah is forever documented in history for his disobedience, bad attitude, and poor example of what it means to be a believer.

I'm grateful for the challenge Mr. Levy gave me, because the Biblical lesson I learned from it stayed deep in my heart and taught me much. It taught me to constantly be in check about the condition of my heart.

"Whoever does not love does not know God,
because God is love."
1 John 4:8 (NIV)

What is the condition of your heart? As a believer in Christ, you must constantly remind yourself of what a Christ-like heart would be like in all situations. You will find you need to repent, often. We all do, but the desire to be like Christ must be priority above all feelings and emotions. Easier said than done, I know. It is daily growth. Plain and simple, God is love. We are even called to love our enemies. Before we became saved, we were all on our way to hell. Thank God, for His love! May we strive to follow Him, so we can share the undeserved gift of Salvation that we ourselves were offered. We cannot call ourselves true followers of Christ, otherwise.

17

A Warm Embrace

"Hugging: The truest form of giving and receiving."
-Carol "CC" Miller

IN 2013, I OPENED MY FIRST ART GALLERY IN MY
hometown Art District. It was one of eight cottages on a small
corner of town called The Village on High. Across from my cot-
tage was the art studio of Dennis Tawes. He was a true kindred
spirit to me from day one, taking me under his wing and growing
me daily as an artist and person. Dennis' other half's name was
Linda. I remember the first time he introduced me to her. She was
tall, beautiful, and had a glow around her that few people have. It
was electric, and her joy was contagious. The first thing she did
was grab me and hug me. I can truly say I had never been hugged
so tightly and warmly in my life. It was strong and sincere, and
I could actually feel her love through it. It was like she was hugging my soul.

Linda handed those soul hugs out like candy to the people
around her, yet they were never meaningless or routine…it was
always with the greatest of sincerity and true affection. She was
famous for them. People craved them; I know I did. There was

something healing about them. I would always walk away from her embrace feeling rejuvenated. When Linda walked into a room, love surrounded her and exuded from her. It couldn't be unnoticed, and it could not be ignored.

When Linda Allen Tawes left this world, she left an undeniable void. Not just with Dennis, the love of her life, or her two amazing children, the joy of her life; the whole art community and town became dimmer, as her light was something that could never be perfectly duplicated. It wasn't something about her...it was her.

I will always miss my warm Linda embrace.

Hindsight:

To this day, I still smile from ear to ear every time Linda comes to mind. It is amazing the impact something as simple as a hug can have on a person. How impactful it was, feeling love transfer from human to human. It makes me think of how a hug from God must feel. The warmth of His embrace, the safety in it. It is remarkable how He uses us to connect life's most important emotions through simple actions.

"This is the most profound spiritual truth I know: that even when we're most sure that love can't conquer all, it seems to anyway. It goes down into the rat hole with us, in the guise of our friends, and there it swells and comforts. It gives us second winds, third winds, hundredth winds."
-Anne Lamott, *Traveling Mercies*

This world is a dark and messed up place. Until the Lord's return, we must find ways to light it up. I'm not saying you have to go around hugging everyone, but you should seek the Lord in prayer and ask Him to use you in some way to bring joy, warmth, and love to those around you. He will always give you opportunities, and He will take delight in your eagerness to express His love in a unique way. People will see you coming and be excited to receive it!

"And now these three remain: faith, hope and love. But the greatest of these is love."
1 Corinthians 13:13 (NIV)

18
Not Forgotten

**"But my God shall supply all your need according
to his riches in glory by Christ Jesus."
Philippians 4:19 (KJV)**

IN 2008, MY FIRST MARRIAGE ENDED. I HAD THE
intimidating challenge before me of becoming a single mother of
a five-year-old and an infant. All I had ever known up to that point
was unhealthy co-dependent relationships, and my confidence in
myself was not strong. Nevertheless, I knew it would be difficult,
but I had to move forward into a new life for the well-being and
happiness of myself and my children.

I didn't know how I would support the three of us, but the Lord
brought me a job within a week. I didn't know how I was going to
afford a new place to live, but the Lord provided me with my best
friend, Charissa, who completely uprooted herself from her life and
not only helped me find a new house, but moved into the house
with me to help me with bills and the children. He blessed me
with friends who helped with the move and came by, often unan-
nounced, to help us fix it up. He provided me with trustworthy
babysitters, who loved my children sincerely. I had supportive

parents and siblings, who prayed for me, and who filled many voids for the children with their time, love, and teachings. He provided me with counselors who helped in my growth and healing. He sent me extraordinary people from unexpected places to love me and show me that I was special, valuable, and worthy of love (things I had never believed before). He gave me a church family who uplifted me and the children in more ways than I can count.

There were still times that we struggled, times when I didn't know if I would be able to afford groceries or things for the kids. I would talk to the Lord, expressing my needs and fears, and without fail, provision would come. There were several times when I came home from work and there were bags of groceries or packs of diapers just sitting on my doorstep. To this day, I don't know who put them there.

I'll never forget one time when I didn't have enough money to pay the electric bill, and it was already late. Later that week, I started going through my closets and belongings, seeing if there was anything I could sell online or in a yard sale. I found a couple coats that were still nice that I didn't wear anymore, so I pulled them out of the closet and emptied the pockets. To my utter disbelief, inside one of the pockets was the EXACT amount of money that my electric bill was, TO THE CHANGE! It was impossible. It was God.

Hindsight:

At a time, when I was afraid, intimidated, and going through one of the largest changes and heartaches of my life, my Heavenly Father never forgot me. He provided the people, places, and things needed to meet my every need and to fill my every void. He allowed this time to grow me. I had a lot of growing to do. I wasn't a perfect person. I was broken, shattered, and made many mistakes during the transition, but He never abandoned me. He picked me up, dusted me off, and carried me. He took me, an insecure, fragile mess of a human, and over time built me into a confident, strong, independent woman who didn't have to walk through life limping and hurting anymore. That doesn't mean life hasn't had its many excruciating pains and challenges since, but I am able to walk through this imperfect life, knowing God has my back. I don't have to be afraid. I know my Heavenly Father will continue to meet my every emotional, physical, and spiritual need. He's a good, good Father, who will never forget me.

"Have I not commanded you? Be strong and courageous. Do not be afraid; do not be discouraged, for the Lord your God will be with you wherever you go." Joshua 1:9 (NIV)

As a child of the God of the universe, you have nothing to fear. The Bible literally uses the phrases "fear not" and "do not be afraid" 365 times! You have a Father in Heaven who takes delight in protecting and providing for you. He wants you to talk to Him. Share your fears, your worries, your needs. Share everything! You don't have to dress anything up for Him. He is a sounding board who doesn't judge. He just wants you to talk to Him and share your heart. His will is for you to be solely reliant on Him. Surrender it all to Him and watch Him come through for you! Trust that His will for you is good. He loves you with an unfailing love. Just because life doesn't always turn out the way we think it should or the way we wanted, it does not mean we are forgotten. This imperfect world will bring pain and trouble; God has a plan for you through it all. Trust Him! You're His child, and He loves you.

19

Light in the Darkness

"Let your light so shine before men, that they may see your good works, and glorify your Father which is in Heaven."
Matthew 5:16 (KJV)

IN JANUARY OF 2020, MY CHILDREN AND I PARTIC-ipated in the annual Walk for Life event in Washington, D.C., along with 300,000 other like-minded individuals. When I originally asked the children if they wanted to go, I don't think they truly understood the magnitude of the event they were joining. Having me for a mother, none of them were strangers to protests or demonstrations. Together, we have stood against animal circus groups in our community, so I suppose they felt it was going to be similar. You can imagine the astonishment they felt, when they stood on a field, sandwiched between thousands of people, as the President of the United States came out and addressed us all directly.

We marched down the streets of D.C. displaying our signs for the world to see. "Jesus was unplanned too!" read one of ours. We looked around at the endless signs others held around us, finding that some of the holders were abortion survivors, adopted children calling their biological mothers their heroes, and even rape victims stating their children were the greatest joy of their lives. This impacted me deeply, and I could see the overwhelming emotion hiding behind the kids' eyes. We felt like we were part of an army, a Godly army, fighting for the right to life and love of the unborn.

Hindsight:

I was a proud mama that day, watching my little soldiers of Christ stand up tall and courageous among the masses, proclaiming without fear that all life matters! It was one of the most cherished days of my entire life, and I am so glad I got to share it with them. I was overwhelmingly proud to be a human that day. God and truth were represented so well that is was almost impossible not to burst into tears at any given moment, from the sheer admiration of what we were witnessing. The turnout was mind blowing; the experience was life changing. I am so grateful that we live in a country where we have a right to stand up and express what we believe in.

> **"Many times, we think someone is ranting, but they're actually speaking with conviction, and everyone has just forgotten the sound of real passion. We're so afraid of absolutes and a strong gut and digging your heels that we dismiss the powerful voice of a lonely fighter. Listen for quiet strength, for humble confidence. It is not often someone will stand for what is right, what is true, what is pure. More often we're afraid to admit we're afraid because the truth is so blinding in a dark world."**
> **-J.S. Park**

Our platform may not always be large, and our group may not always be numerous. Sometimes, perhaps often, we stand alone.

The important thing is that we stand. We live in a world of darkness. It is our job to be the light in that darkness. Often, we stay quiet, afraid to upset or offend others. In staying dim, we contribute to the darkness. We are called to shine brightly for what is right. How can you personally spark a flame? Once, when passing an animal circus sign in my hometown, I made a comment to the kids about how the treatment of the animals bothered me. "Why don't you do something about it?" one of them asked. I had that moment...that "a-ha" moment. They were right. As young and inexperienced at life as they were, they pulled my card and dared me to do something about what bothered me. They inspired action, and that action ended up causing change. Today, ask yourself what bothers you, and ask the Lord to show you how you can do something about it!

**"Unless someone like you cares a whole awful lot,
nothing is going to get better...it's not."
Dr. Seuss–*The Lorax***

20

Behind the Scenes

**"God is always doing 10,000 things…and you
may only be aware of three of them."
-John Piper**

IT WAS A BEAUTIFUL, SUNNY DAY, IN THE SPRING OF 2019. It was my fourth wedding anniversary, and I was so excited to go out and pick up a gift for my husband while he was at work. I got ready for the day, hopped into the car, and headed toward the mall. I felt the vibration of my cell phone, and smiled, thinking it was Matt sending me a sweet, morning message for the day. It wasn't.

I honestly don't remember what happened for at least an hour after that. I've blacked it out. I remember standing in my mother's driveway as an ambulance pulled in carrying my grandmother, covered in trauma. She was shaking and helpless. "No more Gary," she sobbed as they wheeled her into the house.

My Uncle Gary was a man of few words, but also of great generosity. He and my grandmother shared a house together and visiting them was one of my greatest joys. I always joked with him about how he and I were the black sheep of the family. We had a similar sense of humor and taste in music. He made me laugh and was truly one of my favorite people.

That morning, as my uncle and grandmother were enjoying a cup of coffee together, a junkie ran into the house, assaulted my grandmother, brutally murdered my uncle, robbed the house, and stole my uncle's truck. That was the text I received that morning. That was the morning my family's lives were changed forever.

When I was a kid, I had a dream that my Uncle Gary was standing in his living room facing the front door. His face was lit up, and he looked peaceful and happy. He had a Bible tucked under his arm, held close to his body. In real life, my uncle was very private, and never showed any lean toward any type of religious beliefs. It was difficult to know what he felt or believed about many things. He loved music, that I knew. He loved to garden. He loved to grill. He was the type of man that would give you the shirt off his back if you needed help. These were things that I knew about him, but that deep down inside stuff…he was always a mystery.

When I found out he was stolen from us, I was in obvious grief, sorrow, anger, and disbelief. Even more so, I was greatly concerned. I did not have the peace of knowing if my uncle was in Heaven, and it was killing me on the inside. I loved him so much, and the thought of him being murdered so brutally, only to have an eternity in hell, was more than I could bear.

I spent months very angry at God. In fact, I didn't talk to Him for a while. If I did, it certainly wasn't anything nice. How fortunate we all are that God is big, and His love and compassion is wide enough to keep loving us when we are being the flawed humans we are, temper tantrums and all. He can take it. He can take our anger at Him with grace. He can take our silence with mercy. When I finally got over myself and remembered that I was behaving like a rotten child toward my Heavenly Father, I came to Him with a repentant, but still very broken heart. I expressed to Him how devastated I was to think my uncle may not have been saved.

A short time later, I had the daunting task of helping my mother and sister clean out my grandmother's house. As I made my way to my uncle's room, I made some discoveries I was not prepared for. First, I found a book I had given him for Christmas years before called 'Jesus > Religion' by Jefferson Bethke. It was dog-eared and very used. He read it. This was clear. More amazing than that though, as I opened his closet, I found something taped to the door. It was a blue piece of construction paper with a child's drawing on it. The drawing was a picture of Jesus and the cross, with the Salvation message written under it. It was dated 1992 by Katy Hart. I was ten years old when I drew that. I remember giving it to him. This meant for 27 years, my uncle had this taped to his closet door. 27 years!

I nearly collapsed, not just from the discovery, but from the sheer relief I felt, knowing that this was the Lord's way of letting me know my uncle was safe in His care, the joy of knowing I would see him again, and the small, but much needed, amount of peace I could have in my heart to finally begin the very long task of healing.

Hindsight:

I was tormented by the thought that my uncle suffered such a terrible death, only to end up in eternal pain as well. I prayed for him my whole life. My parents, sister, aunt, and I always shared the truth of Jesus Christ with him, but, as I said, he was very close-lipped on the matter. The burden of having lost him forever was crushing. The Lord spoke so greatly to me through this experience. He reminded me that planting seeds is huge. I didn't pray the sinner's prayer with my uncle, but my whole life, I planted seeds. My parents planted seeds; my sister and aunt planted seeds; my grandmother lived her faith around him. God was watering the seeds in my uncle's heart behind the scenes. He was doing a great and mighty work in him, privately…and that's okay! I thought I needed to SEE my uncle in church, or being greatly outspoken, but I was wrong. The dream I had when I was young was a promise. The picture I found was a confirmation.

I have great peace and joy in my heart, knowing that when I leave this world, my Uncle Gary will be waiting to greet me.

"…God has heard my sobs. My requests have been granted; my prayers have been answered."
Psalm 6:8-9 (MSG)

When someone we love passes away, the knowledge that they are safe in our Heavenly Father's arms brings a comfort like no other. Knowing your separation from that person is only temporary, helps the grieving process become bearable. We miss our loved ones, for sure. The pain is great, and the sorrow is always piercing, but Jesus' sacrifice has given us the promise of tomorrow, beyond the grave.

Do not underestimate the influence you have and the example you set for your loved ones. Pray for them daily and know that God is faithful.

21

Taking Back the Pieces

"Forgiveness is the fragrance that the violet sheds
on the heel that has crushed it."
-Mark Twain

WHEN MY HUSBAND MATT AND I FIRST BECAME
engaged, I was not 100% myself yet. What I mean by that is that I
was still burdened by my past pains and hurts. I was still carrying
around the weight of the emotional, physical, and sexual abuse I
suffered from past relationships and friendships. I was still limping
through life, dragging around the pain that had been caused by
betrayal, lies, and rejection. It may not have always been evident
to others, but I knew. It was deeply internalized. My heart was still
broken...still in pieces. I thought about these things daily.

I brought it to the Lord because I was worried. I was concerned
that my new marriage would be affected, my parenting two new
children would be compromised. I knew I would not be able to
give them everything they all deserved, because I was not whole
myself; parts of me were missing.

The Lord answered me clearly. He said I needed to forgive my
offenders. I did not like that answer. I didn't like it, but I knew it

was true. My feelings of hurt were valid. I was caused great harm. Some of the crimes could only truly be repaid by God. No earthly consequence could be considered true justice. Nevertheless, God was clear; I had to forgive.

I was so in love with my children, my soon to be husband, and my future stepchildren. I wanted to give them everything, not just what I had left. I finally accepted what God was asking of me. I knew He was right. I asked Him to help me forgive my enemies, and I prayed blessings over them. "That's not enough," God said. "You need to tell them that you forgive them." I liked that even less.

I didn't run out the door, seeking all who had damaged me. I did not start a list of people to make phone calls to. I didn't know how or what God had in mind exactly, so I just surrendered and committed to be obedient and trust the Lord's direction. I knew He would guide me and create the circumstances needed for all this to happen.

The list of people wasn't long. There were three. There have been many more than three people that have caused me wounds, but there were three that I drug around with me all the time emotionally...three that still had pieces of me.

The Letter

The Lord had me write a letter to my sexual abuser. I explained in detail what they had done and how it affected my life, how eating disorders and cutting had been ways I tried to deal with it. I expressed how he had killed part of me in a way, how I had attempted suicide twice, haunted by the image of his face. Then I explained how Jesus loved me so much, that for my greatest good, He wanted to free me from the anguish and trauma I had been through, and how the only way He could do that was for me to forgive him, my abuser. I told him he was forgiven. I put a stamp on an unaddressed letter, and I mailed it with no return address. This was the Lord's instructions. This was a way to let it all out, but still stay safe. This was an exercise of obedience.

The Email

I asked the Lord how to express forgiveness to the second person on my list. As they were not a danger, God encouraged me to write out an email and send it to the person, with no expectation of the reply. In obedience, I unburdened my heart, shared my hurt, and offered my forgiveness. I did it all sincerely and without malice. A reply did come, with many excuses and justifications for their actions. They didn't believe they had anything to be sorry for. The Lord reminded me that I need not pay any attention to the reply. This person and I had different views of the truth and lived on different spiritual and moral planets. I wasn't seeking resolution. I was seeking the restoration of my broken heart by releasing that person and what they had done.

The Conversation

The last person was the most difficult. God told me He wanted me to talk to them in person. That was intimidating to even think about. There was a sense of safety in letters and emails. I could hide behind them, in a way. I was nervous and confused as to how the opportunity would even present itself, but God is God, and He orchestrates all things that are within His Will, if we are seeking to please and obey Him. He later created a situation where the person was available in a public setting. When I saw them, I felt God lift me out of my seat. "Hey! Do you have a quick minute?" I shouted. God just took over. The person turned and came toward me. I felt the Holy Spirit guiding my words as I began to speak,

"You don't have to say anything back. I just wanted to tell you that I have this amazing person in my life that wants to marry me, and I can't offer him everything he deserves. I have two new children coming into my care, and I can't be everything they need me to be. I am in pieces, and to be the best wife and mother I can be, I need to be whole. I need to take all my missing pieces back. You have so many of them. I need you to know that I forgive you for everything. All of it. I forgive you for everything you've done, for everything you are doing, and for everything you might do in the future. I am taking my pieces back. I also ask you to forgive me for anything I have ever done on my end. I am truly sorry. Please forgive me."

I didn't get anything in return at that moment. It was a one-sided conversation. I spoke, they listened, and when I was done, we parted ways. But as I walked away, that very moment, I felt years of hurt and bondage just fall off me. I felt ten tons lighter. I felt freedom. I felt whole.

Hindsight:

I have learned through this experience, and many others in my life, that forgiveness is a decision, not a feeling. Forgiveness is freeing one's self of the baggage and moving forward without the ghosts of the past whispering in your ear. I allowed myself to be haunted and crippled for years, holding onto the idea that I had a right not to forgive. I had yet to realize that by walking in unforgiveness I had ignorantly ignored the fact that Jesus Christ, who was abused and tortured for my own sin, hung on His cross begging His Heavenly Father to forgive us, to forgive me. Ouch! I think about all the years I spent pushing good people away, in fear of what they could do to me. I spent years attacked with anxiety and depression. These are years I can never get back.

"Summing it all up, friends, I'd say you'll do best by filling your minds and meditating on things true, noble, reputable, authentic, compelling, gracious – the best, not the worst; the beautiful, not the ugly; things to praise, not things to curse. Put into practice what you learned from me, what you heard and saw and realized. Do that, and God who makes everything work together, will work you into His most excellent harmonies."
Philippians 4:8-9 (MSG)

Friend, I do not know what you have been through, but the Lord does. He knows every crack of your broken heart, and longs to help heal you. He will never be able to do that if you don't surrender all of the hurt to Him. Lay it all at the foot of the cross. Forgive others, forgive yourself, and even forgive God, if you've been angry at Him. You cannot be hearers of the Word only. In order to live a life of peace and joy, you must be a doer of the Word. The Lord gave me a personal strategy on how to walk the road to forgiveness. Seek Him for yours!

"When it comes to forgiveness Jesus set the bar and He set it high!"
-Barbara Hart

22
Searching

"But seek first his kingdom and his righteousness, and all
these things will be given to you as well."
Matthew 6:33 (NIV)

OVER THE COURSE OF 20 YEARS I HAD A RECURRING
dream. It came to me at least once a month. It was always the same...

I was completely alone.

*I walked down cement stairs into a basement. It was set up
like a large underground prison. Everything cement, everything
grey. It was cold and damp. Single light bulbs with pull strings
hung from the ceiling.*

*Instead of cells, there were identical doors, all closed. They
ran down both sides of the basement, and across the back, in a
"U" formation.*

*There was a square hole in the center of the room, cut flat into
the floor, another set of stairs going down from it.*

*I went to each room one at a time. There were dozens of them.
Every door looked the same, but each room had something completely different on the inside.*

Examples:

One was full of antiques; one was set up like a grocery store; one was an arcade; one was full of junk, etc.

I very thoroughly and intentionally looked through everything in each room. I touched every item. It was as if I was searching for something specific, but I never actually knew what it was. I just kept moving on to another room, because I had not found it.

Suddenly, I had an overwhelming sense that I was not alone. I came back out to the main basement, and I felt shaken, heard voices, and could tell people were headed down to where I was.

I became very afraid and frantically headed toward the center of the room, squeezed myself into the hole cut into the floor, and headed down the small staircase inside. I came to a small door at the bottom, pried it open, and went inside, blockading the doorway immediately.

I looked around and found myself in a pure white room. It looked like a sports locker room. Everything was white; everything was clean. It was extremely bright. There were lockers, tile floors/walls/ceiling, showers, and benches. I felt very safe and very warm. I felt peace because I knew I found what I was looking for.

The daily visitation of this dream sequence was astounding. It never changed. It began when I was about 12 years old. By age 32, I was quite studied and grown in prophetic dream interpretation, which is one of my spiritual gifts. The Lord often speaks to me in dreams and visions; He always has. Sometimes He gives me the answers right away, and other times He makes me wait. I felt I knew for a long time what this dream meant, but when I would ask Him for confirmation, He didn't answer, and the dream just kept coming. I must have just been missing something, I thought.

Finally, before my 33rd birthday, I had the dream for the last time. Once a couple of months went by, I asked the Lord one more time for confirmation, and He answered.

Interpretation:

The basement/prison = the world

Me = a person's personal journey

The doors = all the things the world has to offer -religions, relationships, material objects, entertainment, etc.

Searching through and touching everything = all the ways a person tries to find happiness, completion, peace, love, satisfaction.

Sensing other people coming = wanted to be separate from them.

Running to the center = desperation.

Going down the stairs = digging deeper.

Squeezing through the tiny doorway = taking a narrow road.

The white locker room = purity–a place of cleansing. Salvation. Our life after Jesus.

Feeling of peace and warmth = spiritual growth and security. Where I belonged.

Found what I was looking for = something deeper than this world has to offer.

I was thrilled to finally get confirmation. I thought it was a beautiful and profound meaning. I loved it. My confusion was about why He gave it to me so many times! That's really what I wanted to know more than anything.

Hindsight:

Looking back, I know that the Lord had been trying to reach me since I was a young girl about the dangers of searching for fulfillment in all the wrong places. He was calling me out of the world and away from its deceptions. I struggled most of my young life to find my happiness through unhealthy people, substances, worldly experiences, and things. I was left empty every time. There wasn't a person, place, or thing on planet Earth that was ever going to fill the void in my soul. It all led me to nothing. I believe the Lord kept the dream in my life to reinforce this lesson to me, until my life and my spiritual growth were strong enough to completely accept it, when I was choosing to live in the light. How grateful I am to have a Father in Heaven who loves me enough to remind me of such an invaluable truth…to chase me with it. I know without a doubt, this world has nothing to offer. I learned it the hard way. True fulfillment has only come to me through Salvation and my relationship with Jesus Christ.

"When God gives you a new beginning, it starts with an ending. Be thankful for the closed doors. They often guide us to the right ones."
-Aisha Ismael

The greatest thing I could ever share with you is how important it is for you to stay focused on your relationship with Jesus. He is the only source of peace for your soul and spirit.

When we lose focus and start looking to other people or things, we will be disappointed every time. Your spouse cannot complete you. Your children will not complete you. Your friends will not complete you. People are flawed; they let us down. We are all imperfect humans; it's just in the cards. Our creator NEVER lets us down. His plans for us are perfect, and His love for us in unending.

Material things only bring temporary pleasure. Think about celebrities who have endless money with more earthly pleasures and luxuries than most of us could ever dream of; many have had a tragic end.

Stuff isn't enough!

Many people have drug, alcohol, or sex addictions, trying to fill the inner void, but they end up hollower than they began, piling up more baggage, and creating more pain for themselves.

It's all meaningless.

Only when we surrender our everything to God will we find ourselves complete.

"To seek Christ does not narrow one's life. Rather, it brings it to the level of highest possible fulfillment."
-A.W. Tozer

23

Ready for Battle

"A father doesn't tell you that he loves you, he shows you."
-Dimitri the Stoneheart

IN THE SPRING OF 2015, MY HUSBAND AND I WERE
excited to be attending a big convention up in Northern New
Jersey with my good friend Sam. It was similar to a Comic-Con.
We looked forward to the event every year. This particular year,
we were extra excited because Sam's young son Hunter was going
to be joining us for the first time! The Cosplay planning was so
exciting (choosing, designing and putting together a standout costume to wear). Attendees spend the day wearing their creations
and admiring everyone else's.

Sam came to our house the night before the show so we could
all work on costumes together. He was creating a Black Panther
costume for Hunter. I was especially impressed with his creative
efforts that year. Sam doesn't buy stuff; he makes it. A true artist,
he always puts his heart and soul into everything. I am always in
awe of him.

We had to get up early the next morning for the long drive to
the event, so around 11pm my husband and I headed to bed. Sam

could have called it a night as well. What he had made was good, and it would have worked out fine, but he refused to go to bed. He wanted it to be perfect. He worked all night, making sure the facemask, gloves, bodysuit, shoes, and weapons were embellished and painted perfectly. Every detail was well thought out and with purpose. He took his time creating each piece to fit perfectly and be used effectively.

He slept in the car on the ride to the convention in the morning, exhausted, but pleased and proud of what he created for his little boy. He wanted Hunter to stand out. He wanted people to be impressed with the pieces he made so thoughtfully, and for his child to feel his love through the carefully made head-to-toe pieces prepared just for him.

Little Hunter entered the convention looking like a million dollars. The smile on his face the whole day was a joy to watch. A father's love is a powerful thing.

Hindsight:

When I think back on that day, it reminds me of how our Heavenly Father loves us. He has literally made us head-to-toe pieces of a spiritual costume that makes us stand out…our armor.

The helmet of Salvation – to keep us eternity focused and to give us the mind of Christ.

The breastplate of righteousness – to guard our hearts against direct attacks.

The belt of truth – to fight without being hindered.

The shoes of the gospel of peace – to stand firm in Christ alone.

The shield of faith – to use offensively and defensively.

The sword of the spirit – to know, speak, and use the Word of God.

"Put on the full armor of God, so that you can take your stand against the devil's schemes. For our struggle is not against flesh and blood, but against the rulers, against the authorities, against the powers of this dark world and against spiritual forces of evil in the heavenly realms. Therefore, put on the whole armor of God, so that when the day of evil comes, you may be able to stand your ground, and after you have done everything, to stand. Stand firm then, with the belt of truth buckled around your waist, with the breastplate of righteousness in place, and with your feet fitted with the readiness that comes from the gospel of peace. In addition to all of this, take up the shield of faith, with which you can extinguish all the flaming arrows of the evil one. Take the helmet of Salvation and the sword of the spirit, which is the Word of God. And pray in Spirit on all occasions with all kinds of prayers and requests. With this in mind, be alert and always keep on praying for all the Lord's people."
Ephesians 6:10-18 (NIV)

Our Father in Heaven knew what we would need to both stand out from the world and defend ourselves against it. He provided us with armor for the battle of life. He created us to be a holy army, fully dressed in His divine protection. Make sure you put on each piece every day with pride and gratitude for the sacrifice that He made to make sure you were ready. Allow that knowledge to remind you of what a loved child of God you are.

24

The Paths of Testimony

"Your story is the key that can unlock someone else's prison."
-Kenneth Hagee

ONE OF THE GREATEST MOMENTS OF MY LIFE, EMO-
tionally and spiritually, was the day I had my first major book
signing/reading after the release of *'Pieces of an Abstract Hart'* in
2018. It was my first solo publication, and it was very personal. A
collection of poetry I had written from ages 16-36, there was a
roller coaster journey to share of the worst and best times of my
life, and everything in between. Having an audience to read the
work to was very different from having people read the book privately. It was a spotlight.

My parents and sister were attending. This made me nervous
as well, for I had yet to share some of the contents of the book with
them. There were things they were going to learn about me that I
had spared them from up to that point.

I prayed a lot before it started, "Give me courage, Lord. Please
help this testimony bring honor to You and use it to help anyone
it can." I felt peace, and the Holy Spirit guided me through the
reading. I read the poems and shared the stories behind them.

I revealed the scars of abuse, betrayal, regret, depression, and self-hatred. I laid out the ugliness with as much transparency as the Lord provided grace for. Later, I transitioned into the shifts in my life that caused it all to change direction…the way that God chased me down and put me back together piece by piece, how He was always the answer to the restoration of my life.

As I stripped down and stood emotionally and spiritually nude in front of an audience of loved ones, colleagues, and strangers, I felt a peace that surpasses all understanding. I felt a freedom that I had never felt before. I no longer had to keep the pains or joys of my life hidden. At that moment, I felt more comfortable in my own skin than I ever had before.

The reading led to a time of discussion with the audience afterward. I stood in awe of the Lord as He opened the hearts of people to share their own similar experiences, things they felt safe to share for the first time because they saw someone else have the courage to do it. I receive no glory in this; it was all God.

It was a very diverse group of people that came to hear me read that day. An eclectic collection of religions and beliefs, yet they all listened to me with respect, and supported me after with love. I was blessed and overwhelmed by their responses, and I felt comfortable being myself.

When I went home that night, I thanked the Lord for the opportunity to use my story to encourage others. I resolved at that moment that all the regrets of the past were gone. If I had to have gone through everything I did to be where I was now, it was all worth it. It was no longer my mess; it was my message.

Hindsight:

There have been many times throughout my life when I have struggled with feelings of regret, wondering what my life may have been like if I had not made so many mistakes. All the plans and dreams I had as a kid were certainly not what my foolish decisions led to. My disobedience to my parents growing up, my infatuation with boys, my involvement with worldly friends...it all took me down a painful, drama-filled path. How many tears did I not have to cry? How many times could my heart have been spared the brokenness? How different would things look? Most of my 20's I felt that way. My mind would struggle with self-pity and all the "what ifs."

There was a huge shift in my life when I turned 30. My relationship with the Lord was restored and growing every day. I no longer kept Him at arm's length, I embraced Him. I desired Him. I always knew He was real, but much of my younger years, I didn't always feel like He loved me. I understand that was never the case. I didn't love me; that was the true reality. Once I had a mature understanding of what the truth was, I was able to let go of the regret and the self-pity. I was able to accept my responsibility in parts of my past circumstances (disobedience, living like the world, etc.), and mutually have a deep inner healing in realizing that many of the things (especially the abuse) were not my fault.

Once I was done trying to control my own life, once I was done keeping God at a distance, everything changed. Once I surrendered, He immediately set me back on the path that was always meant for me, the path that led me to my passions, career, and ministries. It walked me right into the arms of the love of my life, creating my beautiful blended family. It healed my relationship with my parents; it kept me very picky about my close circle of friends. This path that was always meant for me, led me to a love for myself.

My life was restored.

"Enter through the narrow gate. For wide is the gate and broad is the road that leads to destruction, and many

enter through it. But small is the gate and narrow is the
road that leads to life, and only few find it."
Matthew 7:13-14 (NIV)

"Whether you turn to the right or to the left, your ears will
hear a voice behind you, saying, "This is the way; walk in it."
Isaiah 30:21 (NIV)

You are not stuck. Your Heavenly Father, who loves you with
an unfailing love, has not abandoned you because of your mistakes. You may be on the wrong path, but He is willing and ready
to guide you back the right way if you surrender your life to Him.
He is faithful and just to forgive you and restore all of the lost
dreams of your heart. Your story can still be a beautiful testimony
of God's unfailing love, and your past experiences can be used
to help those still on the road to destruction. It can all be used.
Nothing is wasted.

25

Dancing in the Rain

"God promises to make something good out of the storms
that bring devastation to your life."
Romans 8:28 (Paraphrased)

THE SUMMER OF 2016, MY HUSBAND, MY BEST
friend Charissa, and my friends Matt, Sea, Kathy, and Jim were all
meeting in Camden, New Jersey to see Bob Dylan and his band,
live in concert. We were so excited! My hubby, Charissa and I were
driving up together to meet everyone else there. About halfway
through the trip, a terrible storm started. Rain was coming down
so hard it was difficult to see where we were going; it was coming
down so fast that it caused flash flooding.

So, there we were on the highway, with bumper to bumper
traffic, at a standstill. We were all in good spirits but were beginning
to be concerned about making it to the show on time. Eventually,
water began to fill the road, and people began panicking. Some
people drove their cars across the grass to the opposite side of the
highway. Others, like us, managed to back up and jump the curb,
cutting through to the nearest offramp that we had just passed.

We thought we were in the clear at this point, but traffic was still slowed down by many accidents. It took us what felt like forever to get there. We arrived late, but we arrived! We met up with my other friends and made our way to the field to put our chairs down and get ready to watch a legend take the stage! The rain had stopped at this point, and we felt relieved to get to watch the show in peace.

Suddenly, the moment of calm was over, and the skies again began pouring unforgivingly down on us. How could this be happening after everything we had already gone through?! It wasn't fair! At that moment, Bob Dylan and his band took the stage. The seven of us looked around at each other and burst into laughter! We ended up splashing and dancing in the rain through the whole concert. It was so much fun! We decided to make it fun!

The day was challenging to say the least. Every time we thought nothing else could go wrong, it did. It would have been so understandable for us to have just gone home, gotten angry or merge into a bad mood, but instead we chose to stay positive and not allow our day to be ruined. We stayed focused on the goal, to listen and watch one of the greatest poets and musicians of all time, and we did just that. The show was going to go on, with or without us.

Hindsight:

My life has been a long list of storms. Many times, I felt like I was going to drown or be swept away. Thankfully, God has always been there for me as a source strength and has brought me through each one with a testimony to share. Insecurity, abuse, loss, betrayal, sickness, financial struggle, divorce, unemployment, rejection, accusation…you name it! Sometimes it didn't just feel like a storm; it felt like a hurricane with tornadoes and tsunamis all at once! When I didn't have my eyes focused on Him and His Word, like

Peter on the water, I sank. But if my focus was purely on God and His promises, I felt Jesus walking beside me on the waters.

When I wouldn't stand on God's Word, like a house built on the sand, I would fall.

> **"But Jesus immediately said to them:**
> **"Take courage! It is I. Do not be afraid."**
> **"Lord, if it's you," Peter replied,**
> **"tell me to come to you on the water."**
> **"Come," he said.**
> **Then Peter got out of the boat, walked on the water and came toward Jesus. But when he saw the wind, he was afraid and, beginning to sink, cried out, "Lord save me!"**
> **Immediately Jesus reached out his hand and caught him.**
> **"You, of little faith, he said, "why did you doubt?"**
> **Matthew 14:27-31 (NIV)**

God has never promised us that life would be easy. In fact, He assured us we would have trouble. He does, however, promise that He is greater than any storm we face. This imperfect world is only our temporary dwelling place, and we must keep that in mind as we daily walk through the monkey wrenches and unexpected storms thrown our way. When we keep our focus on God's promises, we can handle anything and still appreciate, even enjoy, our imperfect life.

Don't let the storms rob you of your joy. Stand firmly on the rock. Remember, God gave us the rainbow as a sign and promise that we would come through the storm victorious. God sends showers of blessings as well.

Dance in the rain, my friend.

"Everyone then who hears these words of mine and does them will be like a wise man who built his house upon the rock. And the rain fell, and the floods came, and the winds blew and beat the house, but it did not fall…"
Matthew 7:24 (ESV)

26

Caged by Fear

"Extreme fear can neither fight nor fly."
-William Shakespeare

BEING A HUGE ANIMAL ACTIVIST, SOME OF MY MOST treasured memories would have to be protesting animal circuses with my children, Christian and Kairi. We would hold signs for hours at the entrances of the events. We would hand out literature and talk to the people passing by about how the animals were trained. Many people would just walk by and ignore us, looking too forward to the entertainment aspect of the show to even give a second thought to what it meant for the animals. However, there were several people who would stop and listen to us, educating themselves on the training process and the daily life of the big cats and elephants, in particular.

When we showed them the way the animals were "broken" by fear at a young age in order to submit to the training, they would tear up. They simply had no idea. Elephants, for example, are tied down and pulled by all four limbs as babies. This inability to move trains them to believe that any time something is secured to their ankles, they will not be strong enough to pull away. All of the tricks they perform are things they were forced to learn through fear of the bullhook's hit or the electric shock's sting, both used on their delicate skin until they submit.

Because of the trauma they are put through, these mighty creatures forget they are strong. Fear paralyzes them. Fear keeps them living in small cages. Fear dictates their every move and action.

Without that fear, elephants could crush anything in their way. Tigers and lions would devour their trainers. They would know that they do not belong in a cage, dancing on boxes and jumping through hoops at the command of something so much weaker.

Hindsight:

The Lord has used my experiences fighting for these animals to teach me something even deeper about my own life. For most of my younger life, I too was living in a cage. Restrained by anxiety and insecurity, I didn't believe in myself and stayed far too long in relationships and situations that were abusive and unhealthy for me. I had become trained to believe that I didn't deserve more and that I was too weak to walk away and make it on my own. I fell into a false sense of reality.

When I was 27 years old, He gave me a dream:

I was in a small, cold, damp room. It was a prison cell with bars on the single window to the outside. I was naked and shivering. Everything inside the cell, including myself, was black and grey.

I walked to the window and looked outside. Everything was in bright vivid colors. Grass covered hills, and tall blooming trees in lovely shades of green. The sky was crystal blue, and the sun was shining. People were walking, and children were playing. Everyone looked so peaceful and happy.

I wanted out. I felt desperate to feel the warmth of that sun on my face. I ran to the door, but it was locked. I banged on it as hard as I could, tears streaming down my face.

Suddenly, a dark figure of a faceless man threw the door open and pushed me back. I was terrified of him.

He proceeded to urinate across the doorway, and then slammed the door shut, leaving me shaking on the floor.

I looked down, and in my arms was a faceless child. Somehow, I knew that it was me. I was holding myself. I wept and rocked my lifeless younger self, like a mother in mourning. I didn't want her to die. I didn't want to lose myself.

My loving Heavenly Father was giving me an eye-opening depiction of my life and how fear was keeping me from moving on and away from the people and things that were not good for me. Until I was willing to cast the fear aside and believe I was the strong, brave, and courageous woman He created me to be, I would always remain in a prison of my own making.

> "For God has not given us a spirit of fear,
> but of power and love and of a sound mind."
> 2 Timothy 1:7 (KJV)

Most of us are just like exotic animals in the circus; caged by fear, we live limited lives. It is the devil's favorite way to cripple us from the great callings God has for our lives. He uses fear to make us believe we are weak, because he himself is terrified of how strong we were made to be in God's kingdom. How ironic that the devil uses fear against those who make him afraid.

> "Fear has a large shadow, but he himself is small."
> -Ruth Gendler

27

When Angels Fly Away

"I have seen and met angels wearing the disguise of
ordinary people living ordinary lives."
-Tracy Chapman

WHEN I WAS AT MY FIRST ART STUDIO, MY CHIL-
dren played outside within the safety of the eight cottages that
circled flower-lined pathways and decorative benches. One of the
cottages, An Octopus's Garden, was owned by Mike and Maryann
Kuntz. You had to know them to understand, but they were the
embodiment of love and everything it stands for. My daughter
Trinity was only five at the time, so if I couldn't keep close watch,
I would have her inside the studio with me. My son Matthew was
about ten, so he could play within the confines of the small village circle on his own. The thing about Matthew is that he, by
nature, was a loner. It was not just a characteristic of his personality, but additionally a symptom of his mild autism. He did not
connect with people easily, especially adults. He normally would
run around the paths outside, line up all of this little GI Joe figures
and miniature toys on the benches, or lay out and display his hand

drawn paper men on the tables for the passersby to see. He played and lived mostly in his own little world and was happy to do so.

You can imagine my surprise when one day, through my studio window, I heard him having a conversation with someone…like a real conversation. I peeked my head out the door to find Matthew on a bench with Mike Kuntz. I watched as Mike got down on Matthew's level and started asking him questions about his paper men. Matthew was engaged in the conversation, answering all of Mike's questions about who the paper men were and what made them special. Matthew's face lit up as he explained them each with passion.

Throughout my time at the village, my heart grew every time I would watch Mike purposefully come out to play with and talk to my son. "I can't wait to show Mr. Mike my new paper man!" he would say on the drive into town. Matthew would even bring his special Superman figures because he knew Superman was Mr. Mike's favorite.

Their connection was remarkable to me. Mike was always so gentle and so attentive in his approach. My son was drawn to him in a way I had never seen before and that I have not seen since.

You can imagine the devastation we felt, when Mike was called home to be with the Lord in 2016. Finding the right words to tell my son about Mike's passing was beyond difficult. I tried to be as gentle as possible, but delivering the news to a little boy, that he would not be able to visit his special friend anymore, was overwhelming. I needed a lot of strength from the Lord. He cried a lot. He asked me if Mr. Mike was now an angel. "I think he already was," I said in reply. I shared the following quote with him to bring him some comfort:

"God always send angels in your life in the form of human beings. Don't feel sad when it is time for them to

**leave you. They were sent to you for a mission. To make
you strong. To build your confidence. To not let you fall
or end up being miserable for a lifetime. When their task
is complete, they leave you to help others. So always be
grateful for the time they spent with you."
-Lourdes Alexander**

He smiled through his tears and ran off to his room. When
he came out, he brought me a picture he had drawn. It was of Mr.
Mike in a Superman costume. I praised him for how special it was.
Emotions melted me as he made the most beautiful statement I
have ever heard a child say:

"I know angels have wings, mommy, but I think God gave Mr.
Mike a cape instead."

The very next time we went to the village, he gave the picture
to Mike's wife, Maryann. It was so special to her. It hangs in An
Octopus's Garden to this day.

Hindsight:

Losing a loved one is never easy. Losing Mike, the angel in
my son's life, was beyond words. Three years. It doesn't seem like
enough. Looking back, regardless of the amount of time, I know
that I am forever grateful for the brief, yet impactful, love and connection that was made between him and my boy.

It wasn't the amount of time; it was the quality of it.

I thank Jesus for the gift of Mike Kuntz.

**"He will wipe every tear from their eyes. There will be
no more death or mourning or crying or pain, for the
order of things has passed away."
Revelation 21:4 (NIV)**

Today, reflect on the gratitude you feel for the "angels" in your life, past or present. Thank your Heavenly Father for loving you enough to send them to you. If they are living, hold them tighter. If they are in Heaven, smile, for one day you'll see them again. This is the promise we have as believers.

"When you miss someone, you remember them, and one day it will make you smile."
Clara – *The Nutcracker*
(film, 2018 - screenplay by Simon Beaufoy)

28

True Royalty

> "But you are a chosen people, a royal priesthood.
> A holy nation, God's special possession, that you
> declare the praises of him who called you out of
> darkness and into his wonderful light."
> **1 Peter 2:9 (NIV)**

ARIZONA HAS ALWAYS BEEN ONE OF MY FAVORITE places on earth. I am obsessed with the desert, the red rocks, the cactus, the warmth. My parents took me there for the first time when I was ten years old. I've been back about a dozen times since. Born a Jersey girl, I am a desert flower at heart.

The most recent visit was in October of 2019. My husband Matt and I decided our children were the right ages to appreciate a vacation to Grand Canyon National Park, the Antelope Canyons, Sedona, and Phoenix. We were so excited to have them experience the Godly creativity and magnitude of everything these places held.

Along our drive from Sedona to the Grand Canyon, we stopped along the road when we saw the Navajo tribes set up with goods to sell. I have always had a heart for the Navajo people, supporting and talking with them at every opportunity.

As I perused each table of exquisitely handmade jewelry, I came across a tiny card table where a beautiful little girl was seated. She was around seven or eight years old. Her table was filled with bathroom tiles, and she was decorating them with marker drawings and Lisa Frank stickers. I got down on her level and showered her with praise over her beautiful creations. I selected two of the tiles and told her to name her price.

"$2 each," she said in a glum voice.

"Why so blue?" I ask her.

"I used to be a real princess, but I'm not anymore," she replied with sadness.

"Oh yeah? Well, I am sorry to hear that. I don't know how being a princess in your culture works, but I do know an artist when I see one, and you are a remarkable artist!" I said to try to cheer her up.

She gave me a half smile, took my $5 and went back to her drawing. What she said had confused me, and I felt so sorry for her because she was so upset. Her grandmother, who was standing nearby, had heard our whole exchange.

"Don't mind her," she said.

"I don't mind at all; I just didn't know what to say," I replied.

She went on to tell me that in their culture, every year, a child at school is chosen to be a princess for a year. They have a big ceremony and everything. Last year, her granddaughter was the princess, and now that school had recently restarted, she had to surrender her title to the newly chosen girl (which she wasn't taking very well, obviously).

When I finished up my shopping, I went back to the car, but I didn't drive away. I was really bothered by how sad the girl was. I reached under my seat and grabbed the gallon sized Ziplock bag filled with quarters that we always had with us for emergencies. I got out of the car and headed back over to the little girl's table. She was surprised to see me again. I asked her if I could talk to her for just a second. With her grandmother's permission, she came over and we had a chat.

"I think you undercharged me for your tiles," I said.

"No, ma'am, you gave me a dollar too much," she replied.

"Well, little princess, I am an artist too, and I have a very good eye when it comes to how much someone's work is worth. These tiles are so beautiful. So, I'll tell you what…you can charge other people anything you want to, but I am going to pay you what I feel like they are worth to me. Does that sound okay?"

She looked at me with uncertainly as I pulled the large heavy bag of quarters out of my purse. Her eyes got wide as saucers. Suddenly, two other young girls came running over with excitement to see the treasure their friend just received. She looked up at me with a huge smile and wrapped herself around me in a hug so precious I could never forget it. As I went to leave, I got down on her level and whispered in her little ear, "You will always be royalty to me."

Hindsight:

That Arizona vacation is, to date, by far my favorite. Matt and I shared unforgettable moments with our children that we will all hold deep in our hearts until the end of time. I have to say though, my encounter with this little Navajo princess, will stay with me equally as long.

When I reflect on the way she felt "less than" because someone else was now in the spotlight, it makes me think about how we are all in some way struggling with the status of our own lives. As kids, we compete in athletic, artistic, and academic things. When we win, we feel on top of the world. When we lose, we often feel discouraged and like we don't measure up. As adults, it's often the level of our education, our careers, the size of our houses, or the cost of our cars that we internally compare to others.

I was guilty of this in the past about my artwork. I have often found myself looking at another artist's work and noticing myself entertaining emotions of insecurity, questioning my abilities. What I have come to realize over the years is that comparison is a tool that Satan uses to torment us. He laughs at us while we feel "less than."

"Comparison is the thief of joy."
-Theodore Roosevelt

The bottom line is, we cannot allow ourselves to become envious and bitter at the talents, success, awards, or titles given to others. We are all royalty in the Kingdom of God. He created us all with gifts and abilities. Our platforms may be different, and our roles may change, but that means nothing in God's eyes. It holds no truth to your worldly or eternal value.

On the days we are on top, may we shout praises to the Lord for His blessings. On the days someone else is getting the recognition, may we humble ourselves and be happy for them! It is okay for other people to shine! If we remember that we are all sons and daughters of the King of the universe, we can live a life of joy as one powerful, royal family. Put that chin up and fix your crown!

"God's kingdom is already among you."
Luke 17:21b (MSG)

29

In Need of Rescue

"Then they cried to the Lord in their trouble, and He saved
them from their distress. He sent out His Word and healed
them; He rescued them from the grave."
Psalm 107:19-20 (NIV)

IN 2007, I ENTERED THE DOORS OF OUR LOCAL
animal shelter to see a litter of Pitbull puppies that had been adver-
tised in the paper. My son was five years old, and it seemed like a
great time to get him a new friend. By the time I arrived, all but
one puppy were already gone. It was a little male puppy, but I could
tell from his personality that he was not the right pet for our home.
In disappointment, I started to leave, when I noticed the mother
dog shaking in the corner of the kennel next to his. She looked
terrified and in poor condition.

I went and found a worker and started asking questions about
her. It was revealed to me that the intention was to euthanize her
after the last puppy was adopted because of her severe health
issues and poor body condition. It broke my heart to hear this, so
I asked her what could be done to help with her medical issues. She
had a severe upper respiratory infection and was having frequent

asthma attacks. The medication that she needed was very expensive, and her chances of surviving, even with the meds, was minimal. Her lungs were so damaged, they didn't have much hope for her recovery. It was so sad.

I had gone to the shelter that day with a certain amount of money on me to adopt a puppy. I asked the worker, if I was willing to pay for the medication, would they be willing to give her a chance. She went and checked with a supervisor at the front office and came back with the news that they were willing to try. I paid them the amount they needed to order the meds and told them that if she pulled through to give me a call because I was willing to adopt her if she did. Three weeks later, I got the call to come pick her up because she had pulled through the infection!

When we got our new girl home, she was so nervous. You could tell she had no idea what being in a house was like, and she would flinch if we moved too quickly. She was so skinny; you could see every bone in her body. Her skin was flaky and dry, her ears were filled with mites, and her legs were all cut up from dog bites. The shelter believed she was used for breeding and as bait for a dog fighting ring. Life for this poor girl had certainly not been kind.

We named our special girl Lucy. Over the course of the first year, Lucy gained 40 pounds, her cuts healed nicely, and she adapted quickly to her new life of love and gentleness. You could tell she was grateful for her rescue.

Lucy was a staple in my life for 11 years. She filled our home with cuddles and laughter. She was a loyal, well behaved, sweet girl, who filled our hearts with joy. I know we rescued her, but she paid us back with her love far beyond measure.

We sent our Lucy girl over the rainbow bridge in the fall of 2018. She was 16 years old, which is almost unheard of for a Pitbull. She may have had a rough start in life, but once she was rescued, she became the happy, healthy girl she was always meant to be. She passed away knowing she was special. Our love changed her life, and her love changed ours.

> **"I waited patiently for the Lord; he turned to me**
> **and heard my cry. He lifted me out of the slimy pit.**
> **Out of the mud and mire; he set my feet on a rock**
> **and gave me a firm place to stand."**
> **Psalm 40:1-2 (NIV)**

Hindsight:

When I think back on the story of my Lucy girl, I see such a beautiful comparison to how Jesus' love changes our lives. He literally sees our suffering and longs to heal us everywhere we hurt. He doesn't see us as a lost cause or as damaged goods. He sees everything we can be, everything He created us to be. He literally sacrificed Himself to take on our suffering and pain, so that through Him we could be rescued, through the gift of Salvation, to spend an eternity with Him in Heaven, knowing only love and joy.

He does not leave us behind.

> **"God is on the move to rescue people from misery to ever-**
> **lasting happiness which can only be found in Him."**
> **-John Piper**

May you wake up every day with appreciation for a Heavenly Father who looks upon you with compassion. If you are currently in need of rescue, have the courage to reach up and grab His hand. He is waiting to restore and heal you. He loves you with an unfailing love.

30

Meet You at the Gate

"After that, we who are still alive and are left will be caught up together with them in the clouds to meet the Lord in the air. And so we will be with the Lord forever."
1 Thessalonians 4:17 (NIV)

Dream from the Lord, 2019:

I WAS STANDING IN A BEAUTIFUL FIELD FULL OF free roaming farm animals. I was watching white, fluffy clouds float across the beautiful blue sky. It was a perfect day.

Suddenly, the ground began to shake, and the animals started running away, all in the same direction.

I looked back at the sky, and it started to rip open. Blindingly bright light was shining through the tear in the sky.

I knew this was the rapture.

I ran home, and my husband and children were not there. In a panic, I called his cell phone and he answered.

"Where are you guys; do you see this?!" I asked.

"We went out for ice cream," he replied. "We are all okay, and we know what is happening."

"I am so sorry I am not with you guys," I sobbed.

Then he offered the most comforting words I have ever heard: "It's okay, Baby. We love you, and we will meet you at the gate."

I ran to the front of the house and looked out the large bay window. There were people everywhere outside looking up at the sky. Some looked terrified, running away like the animals had. Some held up signs, welcoming what they thought must be aliens. Some stood perfectly still with peaceful faces, looking upon the ripped sky with awe and wonder.

I noticed a little girl about six years old all by herself, crying. She *looked* lost and afraid.

I knew there wasn't much time left, so I ran outside and grabbed her. As I pulled her back into the house with me, I assured her that everything was going to be okay.

We both approached the bay window. As we looked up at the sky, everything turned bright white, and I felt myself lift off the ground, weightless.

When I woke up, my heart was beating so fast. Tears ran down both sides of my face, as the sensation of the weightlessness I had at the end of the dream, continued to linger. The exhilaration was overwhelming; it took me quite a while to calm down. Once I was able to focus, I immediately prayed to the Lord for the confirmation of His divine message. I laid back, and He spoke to me.

Interpretation:

Open field and animals = the earth and all creation.
Sudden shaking = the surprise of the time of the Lord's return.
The animals running = the fear of the Lord.
Running home = worried about my family.
Phone call = connection

My husband's words = assurance of the salvation of our family.
The bay window = seeing the different views of the people.
Little girl = a lost soul.
Pulling her into the house = bringing her into safety.
White bright light = the return of Christ.
Weightlessness = our spirits being called up with Him.

As the Lord revealed the deeper meaning of this unforgettable dream to me, I continued to lie down and weep in His presence and goodness.

Hindsight:

Of the innumerable dreams and visions the Lord has sent me over the years, this was by far my most treasured. It holds within it, the most important knowledge of the universe: the return of Christ being undeniable. I feel blessed beyond measure to know that no matter where I am when this happens, I can meet my husband and children at the holy gates of Paradise. Knowing our Salvation is secure brings a supernatural peace. At the same time, contained in this message was the vital importance of reaching the lost souls of this world. There is always someone who will need to hear the message of Jesus and be brought into the safety of His grace, but our time is short. We do not know what day we will take our final breath, nor do we know the hour of the return of our Lord. We must be on constant watch for those we can save. We only have so much time.

"But of the day and hour knoweth no man, no, not the angels in heaven, but my Father only."
Matthew 24:26 (KJV)

Be encouraged today to seek out the lost people in your life. Your neighbors, co-workers, family members, and friends are all at risk. Tell them the good news of a loving Savior who sacrificed Himself to deliver them from an eternity in hell. Tell them how He longs to heal, comfort, and carry them through the challenges of this imperfect world. Remind them that His perfect love is stronger than anything else they could ever experience.

You only have one life on earth. With the time you are given, your greatest responsibility is to point as many to Salvation as possible. That was Jesus' mission, and that is the mission He left to those of us who believe.

Share the good news of Jesus, so that you too can meet the ones you love at the gate!

31

The Only Way

"My eager expectation and hope is that I will not be
ashamed about anything, but that now and always,
with boldness, Christ will be highly honored in my
body, whether by life or death."
Philippians 1:20 (BSB)

IN THIS COLLECTION OF STORIES FROM MY LIFE, I
have shared many hills and valleys with you, some defining
moments, influential people, and life changing outcomes that have
formed the person I am today. The amount of gratitude I feel to
have the opportunity to be transparent with you is beyond words.

My rollercoaster life has had one undeniable truth throughout
– without Christ involved, it was always a hopeless struggle. God's
presence in my life has always been the game changer. Jesus has
always been the answer to everything. Without Him, I was an
empty shell of a human being, longing for life to end. Without
Him I had no strength, no courage, and no direction. Before I
accepted His unconditional love for me, I couldn't love myself. I
was going through the motions but not really living. Pushing Jesus
out of my life was like trying to find my way out of a dangerous

maze blindfolded. Once I took His hand, He not only removed the blindfold, He shined His glorious light to guide my way, picking me up and carrying me when needed.

I prayed the 'Sinner's Prayer' at ten years old, but all my later wounds and poor choices made that Salvation unsecured, not because Christ rejected me for imperfection, but because I willingly rejected Him. The notion of 'once saved, always saved' is simply not true. It is not enough to say the Salvation words, you must truly give your life to Christ and allow Him to be the Lord of your life. You are human, you will make mistakes, but that is why we all needed a Savior to begin with! Jesus is the redeemer of our sins. When we fall, we can ask for forgiveness, and He is faithful and just to forgive us.

How much more could we possibly be loved? The Creator and Master of the universe loved you and me so much that He was willing to send His only Son as a sacrifice for our sins, to save us from an eternity of pain. We did nothing to earn this. He just loves us that much because that is who He is. God is love.

Hindsight:

Looking back at the mess of my past, some could say these things defined me:

-Depression
-Anxiety
-Addiction
-Impurity
-Rage
-Bitterness
-Rejection
-Loss

-Hopelessness
-Insecurity
-Self-Hatred
-Brokenness
-Rebellion

Once I welcomed Jesus into my life, I am now defined by what He says about me:

- I am joyful
- I am peaceful
- I am free
- I am clean
- I am calm
- I am forgiving/forgiven
- I am accepted
- I am comforted
- I am hopeful
- I am secure
- I am loved
- I am whole
- I am a follower of Christ

He took me, a wounded, rebellious, lost soul, and transformed me into a healed, obedient child of God. He brought me full circle, back into the arms of my family, my church body, and the calling and destiny He always had planned for me. He can and will do the same for you. If you were the only person on Earth, He still would have sacrificed Himself just for you. Feel that. Know it. Believe it.

"For God so loved the world that he gave his one and only Son, that whoever believes in him shall not perish but have eternal life."
John 3:16 (NIV)

If you have never invited Christ to be the Lord of your life, or if, like me, you walked away from Him and you would like to find your way back, I invite you to take this moment to surrender your life back to your Creator. He longs for a relationship with you.

Pray the following:

"Jesus, I need You.
I recognize the void in my life that only You can fill.
Come into my heart, Lord.
Heal my broken soul.
Forgive me of my sins.
Help me live a life that follows You.
I believe You died on the cross for the redemption of my sins.
I believe You rose again and are sitting at the right hand of the Father.
I believe You are coming back one day.
I surrender my life to You, Jesus.
In Your name, I pray, amen."

My prayer is that one day, like me, you will look back at your life and be grateful for the testimony you will have to share with others.

We were all lost until we found Jesus. May we share the good news of His love until our last breath!

Praise God.
Amen.

"God did not set us up for an angry rejection but for salvation by our Master, Jesus Christ. He died for us, a death that triggered life. Whether we're awake with the living or asleep with the dead, we're alive with him! So speak encouraging words to one another. Build up hope so you'll all be together in this, no one left out, no one left behind. I know you're already doing this; just keep on doing it."
1 Thessalonians 5:9-11 (MSG)

"I can feel you all around me
Thickening the air I'm breathing
Holding on to what I'm feeling
Savoring this heart that's healing
And so I cry (holy)
The light is white (holy)
And I see You…"

-Flyleaf

CPSIA information can be obtained
at www.ICGtesting.com
Printed in the USA
JSHW030305230720
6829JS00004B/23